KS3 ENGLISH ANTHOLOGY

MYTHS AND LEGENDS

Harmeet Matharu

Series editor: Jane Sheldon

AN HACHETTE UK COMPANY

Although every effort has been made to ensure that website addresses are correct at time of going to press, Hodder Education cannot be held responsible for the content of any website mentioned in this book. It is sometimes possible to find a relocated web page by typing in the address of the home page for a website in the URL window of your browser.

Hachette UK's policy is to use papers that are natural, renewable and recyclable products and made from wood grown in well-managed forests and other controlled sources. The logging and manufacturing processes are expected to conform to the environmental regulations of the country of origin.

Orders: please contact Hachette UK Distribution, Hely Hutchinson Centre, Milton Road, Didcot, Oxfordshire, OX11 7HH. Telephone: +44 (0)1235 827827. Email education@hachette.co.uk Lines are open from 9 a.m. to 5 p.m., Monday to Friday. You can also order through our website: www.hoddereducation.co.uk

ISBN: 978 1 5104 7734 6

© Harmeet Matharu 2020

First published in 2020 by
Hodder Education,
An Hachette UK Company
Carmelite House
50 Victoria Embankment
London EC4Y 0DZ

www.hoddereducation.co.uk

Impression number   10 9 8 7 6 5 4

Year   2024 2023 2022

All rights reserved. Apart from any use permitted under UK copyright law, no part of this publication may be reproduced or transmitted in any form or by any means, electronic or mechanical, including photocopying and recording, or held within any information storage and retrieval system, without permission in writing from the publisher or under licence from the Copyright Licensing Agency Limited. Further details of such licences (for reprographic reproduction) may be obtained from the Copyright Licensing Agency Limited, www.cla.co.uk

Cover artwork by Dylan Gibson http://www.dylangibsonillustration.co.uk/

Illustrations by Integra Software Services Pvt. Ltd., Pondicherry, India

Typeset by Integra Software Services Pvt. Ltd., Pondicherry, India

Printed and bound by CPI Group (UK) Ltd, Croydon, CR0 4YY

A catalogue record for this title is available from the British Library.

Contents

Introduction 3

Fiction 6

1. The Kelpie's Last Battle 6
2. The Odyssey 10
3. King Arthur 14
4. Hercules 18
5. The Ruin of Pennard Castle 22
6. Pan Gu and the Creation of the World 26
7. King Midas and the Golden Touch 30
8. Echo 34

Non-fiction 38

9. The Giant's Causeway 38
10. Mulan 42
11. The Loch Ness Monster 46
12. Robin Hood 50
13. The Beast of Bodmin 54
14. Buffy the Vampire Slayer 58
15. Greek Giants 62
16. Aphrodite 66

Poetry 70

17. The Kraken 70
18. Robin Hood 74
19. The Lady of Shalott 78
20. Near Avalon 82
21. Ulysses 86
22. The Fairies 90
23. Beowulf 94
24. Mrs Midas 98

Key terms 102

The Publishers would like to thank the following for permission to reproduce copyright material.

Acknowledgements

pp. 6–7 Lari Don, from *The Kelpie's Last Battle*, © copyright Lari Don, Scotclans 2008; **pp. 10–11 Joel Skidmore**, from *The Odyssey*, © copyright 1997, 1998 Mythweb. Retrieved from http://www.mythweb.com/odyssey/; **pp. 14–15 Deborah Tempest**, from *King Arthur and the Knights of the Round Table*, 3rd ed., Pearson Education 2000; **pp. 22–23 Graham Watkins**, an Extract from *Welsh Legends and Myths – 80 Myths and Legends from across Wales* by Graham Watkins; **pp. 26–27** © 2008 by Shelley Fu, **Shelley Fu**, *Chinese Myths and Legends: The Monkey King and Other Adventures*, pages 10–14, Tuttle Publishing 2018; **pp. 38–39 Ireland.com**, from 'The Giant Story', TOURISM IRELAND, www.ireland.com; **pp. 42–43 disney.fandom.com**, from 'Mulan (2020 film)'. Retrieved from https://disney.fandom.com/wiki/Mulan_(2020_film). Reproduced under licence CC-BY-SA 3.0 (https://creativecommons.org/licenses/by-sa/3.0/legalcode); **pp. 46–48 John Glover and Tiffany Lo**, from 'Loch Ness Monster hunter films "two 20ft creatures swimming together in water"', MGN Limited. Retrieved from https://www.mirror.co.uk/news/uk-news/loch-ness-monster-hunter-films-18776897; **pp. 50–51 Ben Johnson**, from 'Robin Hood', Historic UK Ltd. Retrieved from https://www.historic-uk.com/HistoryUK/HistoryofEngland/Robin-Hood/; **pp. 58–59 Vanessa Thorpe**, from 'Buffy the Vampire Slayer to be remade 21 years after first episode', *The Guardian*. Retrieved from https://www.theguardian.com/tv-and-radio/2018/jul/21/buffy-the-vampire-slayer-to-be-remade-21-years-after-first-episode; **pp. 62–63 www.amnh.org**, from 'Greek Giants', © American Museum of Natural History; **pp. 94–95, Seamus Heaney**, UK and Commonwealth: *Beowulf* – translated by Seamus Heaney, lines 1–25 2009, FABER & FABER; US: from BEOWULF, translated by Seamus Heaney. Copyright © 2000 by Seamus Heaney. Used by permission of W. W. Norton & Company, Inc.; **pp. 98–99 Carol Ann Duffy**, from 'Mrs. Midas' from *The World's Wife* by Carol Ann Duffy. Published by Anvil Press Poetry, 1999. Copyright © Carol Ann Duffy. Reproduced by permission of the author c/o Rogers, Coleridge & White Ltd., 20 Powis Mews, London W11 1JN.

Photo credits

p. 1 t © Ivy Close Images / Alamy Stock Photo, c © United Archives GmbH / Alamy Stock Photo, b © Keith Corrigan / Alamy Stock Photo; **p. 3** r © Chronicle / Alamy Stock Photo, l © Warner Bros. Pictures /courtesy Everett Collection / Alamy Stock Photo; **p. 4** t © Azoor Photo / Alamy Stock Photo, b © Warner Bros. Pictures / PictureLux / The Hollywood Archive / Alamy Stock Photo; **p. 5** t © Everett Collection Inc / Alamy Stock Photo, b © Chronicle / Alamy Stock Photo; **p. 6** © Dusan Kostic / Alamy Stock Photo; **p. 9** © willyam – stock.adobe.com; **p. 10** © The Print Collector / Alamy Stock Photo; **p. 12** © iveliniliev – stock.adobe.com; **p. 14** © Ivy Close Images / Alamy Stock Photo; **p. 16** © Artem Mazunov – stock.adobe.com; **p. 18** © Rosenwald Collection, 1943.3.5848, Courtesy National Gallery of Art, Washington; **pp. 22 and 25** © leighton collins – stock.adobe.com; **pp. 26 and 29** © Zhang Yongxin/123RF.com; **p. 30** © Historic Images / Alamy Stock Photo; **p. 33** © Dmitriy – stock.adobe.com; **p. 34** © Topham Partners LLP / Alamy Stock Photo; **p. 35** © Azoor Photo / Alamy Stock Photo; **p. 38** © aitormmfoto – stock.adobe.com; **p. 40** © MNStudio – stock.adobe.com; **pp. 42 and 45** © KC Hunter / Alamy Stock Photo; **p. 44** © MARKA / Alamy Stock Photo; **p. 46** © Chronicle / Alamy Stock Photo; **p. 49** © cloudvisual – stock.adobe.com; **p. 50** © Pictorial Press Ltd / Alamy Stock Photo; **pp. 54 and 57** © Helen Hotson – stock.adobe.com; **p. 58** © United Archives GmbH / Alamy Stock Photo; **p. 61** © samiramay – stock.adobe.com; **p. 62** Wiki/Public domain; **p. 65** © trafa - stock.adobe.com; **p. 66** © dudlajzov – stock.adobe.com; **pp. 70 and 72** https://commons.wikimedia.org/wiki/File:Le_Poulpe_Colossal.jpg/public domain; **p. 76** Wellcome Library, London/Creative Commons Attribution only licence CC BY 4.0 http://creativecommons.org/licenses/by/4.0/; **p. 78** © IanDagnall Computing / Alamy Stock Photo; **p. 79** © PAINTING / Alamy Stock Photo; **pp. 82 and 85** © Keith Corrigan / Alamy Stock Photo; **p. 86** © Heritage Image Partnership Ltd / Alamy Stock Photo; **p. 90** © Transcendental Graphics/Getty Images; **pp. 94 and 97** © Ivy Close Images / Alamy Stock Photo; **p. 98** public domain/https://en.wikipedia.org/wiki/File:Midas_gold2.jpg.

Every effort has been made to trace or contact all copyright holders, but if any have been inadvertently overlooked, the Publisher will be pleased to make the necessary arrangements at the first opportunity.

Introduction

Myths and legends are all around us. In every country, there may be a myth about a creature that lives there and terrifies the townsfolk. You may have watched a film where there is a creature that descends from a myth or a legend. What exactly are myths and legends, and why are they so important?

Myths

A myth has more than one definition:
1 An early traditional story, often involving the supernatural. For example, ancient Greek myths.
2 An idea or belief that is false. For example, the belief that carrots help you see in the dark.

NOW TRY THIS

In pairs, write down a list of all of the mythical creatures that you can think of. Examples include unicorns, giants and vampires. When you have finished, share your ideas about mythical creatures with the rest of the class.

▲ A hoaxed photograph of the Loch Ness Monster

In this book, we will be exploring the first definition of a myth – 'a traditional story'. There are lots of traditional stories all around us that are myths, for example the myth of the Loch Ness Monster. The Loch Ness Monster, or Nessie, is a creature that is said to live in Loch Ness in Scotland. Some people claim to have seen it, but there is no definite proof that the monster actually exists. There was a photograph that was taken of the monster in 1934, but now it is known that the photograph is a hoax.

Another mythical creature that you might have heard of is the Yeti. The Yeti, or Abominable Snowman, is said to be an ape-like creature that roams the Himalayan mountains. There have been lots of films about the Yeti, one of the most recent being *Smallfoot* which was released in 2018.

▲ A film poster for *Smallfoot*

Introduction

> **NOW TRY THIS**
>
> What other films can you think of that are about mythical creatures? Share your answers with the rest of the class.

You may have heard of the story of Narcissus. In an Ancient Roman myth, Narcissus was a youth who peered into the water and fell in love with his own reflection. In fact, he loved looking at himself so much that he wasted away and turned into a flower. Nowadays, if we say that someone is 'narcissistic', it means that they admire themselves too much. This myth, like many others, serves as a warning and has a message: don't admire yourself too much because, if you do, something bad could happen to you!

Legends

Unlike myths, legends are based on historical fact. Here are two definitions:
1 A traditional story that many think is based on historical events. For example, 'the legend of Robin Hood'.
2 A person who is extremely famous and well known. For example, 'she was a legend!'

In this book, we will be looking at the first definition of a legend – 'a traditional story popularly regarded as historical but not authenticated'. The legend of King Arthur is a very famous myth that has been made into countless TV programmes, cartoons, comics and films. Historians are unsure about whether King Arthur was an actual king in the late fifth and early sixth centuries. However, by medieval times, there were lots of stories about him and other people who he knew, such as the knight, Lancelot, and the wizard, Merlin. One of the most famous stories involving King Arthur is the Sword in the Stone. According to legend, there was a magical sword placed in a large stone in Westminster, London. On the stone was an inscription:

> 'Whoever pulls the sword from this stone is the rightful king of England.'

Many came from far and wide and found it impossible to pull the sword from the stone. However, Arthur was able to pull the sword from the stone when he was just fifteen.

> **NOW TRY THIS**
>
> In pairs, write down a list of all of the legends that you can think of. Examples include Dracula, Bloody Mary and Robin Hood. When you have finished, share your ideas about legends with the rest of the class.

Another very popular legend that most people in Britain have heard of is the legend of Robin Hood. According to legend, Robin Hood was an outlaw from Sherwood Forest in Nottinghamshire who stole from the rich to give to the poor. His story has become very famous

▲ Narcissus

> **LOOK CLOSER**
>
> Can you think of any other myths that have a moral message?

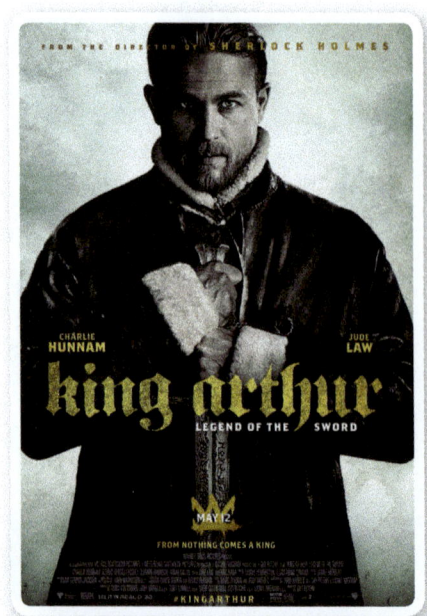

▲ A *King Arthur* film poster

Introduction

and has led to many TV shows and feature films about him. Some historians believe that Robin Hood is based on a real man, Roger Godbeard, who was alive at the same time.

> **NOW TRY THIS**
>
> Many legends have been turned into cartoons and comics. Can you think of any? Share your answers with the rest of the class.

> **WIDER READING SUGGESTIONS**
>
> If you want to find out more about myths and legends, here are some books that you might like to read:
>
> *Norse Myths: Tales of Odin, Thor and Loki*, Kevin Crossley-Holland and Jeffrey Alan-Love
>
> *Treasury of Greek Mythology*, Donna Jo Napoli
>
> *Magical Myths and Legends*, Michael Morpurgo
>
> *Percy Jackson and the Olympians*, Rick Riordan

▲ Disney's Robin Hood

Section 1: Fiction

1 The Kelpie's Last Battle
By Lari Don

▲ A kelpie transformed into a horse

LEARNING OBJECTIVES
- To explain why the writer has made certain language choices (such as the use of emotive language).
- To explain why the writer has made structural choices at both sentence level and whole-text level.
- To see how texts fit into their cultural and historical settings.

CONTEXT
Below is a Scottish myth written by Lari Don, a modern children's author who lives in Edinburgh. It is about the kelpie, a type of monster that lived in Scottish lochs and changed shape when he came on to the shore. Children were warned by their parents that these monsters could often change into a saddled horse. In this particular myth, a crofter's daughter meets a young man who is actually a kelpie. Using her wits, she manages to escape from him.

Don uses the adjectives 'fine' and 'blue' to describe the young man's clothes. Why isn't the young woman suspicious of this man at first?

The young man is friendly as he wants to deceive the woman.

The verb 'struggling' shows how the young man pretends to find combing his hair difficult so that the young woman will help him.

One day, the **crofter**'s daughter was walking along the **loch**. She was, as always, **wary** of saddled horses, but she wasn't concerned when a young man stepped out in front of her. He was dressed in fine blue clothes, had long wild blond hair and a very charming smile.

'Would you do me a favour, young lady?'

'Of course, sir.'

'Would you lend me a comb?'

She had a comb in her apron pocket, so she handed it to him, and he began to get the tangles out of his hair. But he was struggling with the hair at the back of his head, and he raised his eyebrows at her and grinned. 'Would you mind?'

So she sat on the ground, and he lay his head in her lap, and she began to **tease and tug** at the knots in his hair.

Don uses the verb 'wary' to highlight how the crofter's daughter already knows the myth of the kelpies and is aware of how dangerous they are.

The phrase 'very charming smile' also shows us why the young woman decides to be friendly with the young man.

The woman is attracted to the man and is quite comfortable in his presence.

The Kelpie's Last Battle

> The woman is noticing 'odd' things about the man which is making her suspicious.

His hair was a little damp, which was odd, as there had been no rain since yesterday, but ever odder, there was water weed, stringy lumps of green stems and leaves, wound into his hair. That's why it was so hard to comb out.

> The woman is becoming even more suspicious at this point and Don uses the rhetorical question 'water weed in damp hair?' to show this.

Water weed in damp hair? The girl's combing fingers slowed. This wasn't a handsome young man. This must be the beast from the loch, changed not into a horse, but into a man, to try to trick unwary locals under the waves.

Her fingers began to move again. But this time she hummed as she combed, lullabies and love songs, until the man dozed off. She untied her apron, leaving his head upon it as she stood up carefully.

> The young girl is careful. She 'hummed', ensuring the man is asleep before she gets up 'carefully'.

> The alliteration in 'roar of rage' shows how angry the horse is.

She started to run for home. But she heard a roar of rage behind her. Then she heard the sound she had dreaded. Not feet running after her, but hooves. She would never make it all the way back to the croft. Not chased by a four-legged water horse.

> In the story, the crofter has a magical, mythical bull that is angry and violent. The crofter keeps him locked up because he gets angry.

Then she realised she was running past the pen of the fairy bull. She used the comb to flick the latch up and she kicked the pen open and she took cover behind the gate, as the angry black fairy bull stormed out, right into the path of the white water horse.

The bull bellowed, and the horse screamed. And they bit, and they kicked, and they reared, and the kelpie forgot all about the girl, who ran home as fast as she could, the noise of the fight fading behind her.

> Don uses lots of verbs, such as 'bellowed', 'screamed', 'bit', 'kicked' and 'reared' to highlight the anger of the animals.

GLOSSARY

Crofter: a farmer
Loch: a lake
Wary: cautious
Tease and tug: pulling gently at hair
Water weed: weeds that grow in the water
Unwary: not being cautious or careful
Pen: a small area with a fence where an animal is kept
Reared: when an animal raises itself upwards on its back legs

Fiction

SKILLS FOCUS

✔ Understanding how writers create impressions through language and techniques.

✔ Considering how Don's choice of language affects our opinion of the characters.

✔ Exploring how mood, atmosphere and tension are created.

LOOK CLOSER

1. Read the opening of the extract. What do we learn about the young man here? Think about:
   - his appearance
   - his personality
   - the language that Don uses to describe him.

2. Continue reading the extract. Why does the girl become suspicious of the young man?

3. How can we tell that the girl is frightened? What language has Don used to suggest this?

4. How can we tell that the fight between the kelpie and the fairy bull is a violent one? Write a paragraph, with evidence, explaining your answer.

NOW TRY THIS

1. Create your own mythical creature.

My mythical creature			
Name			
Appearance	Face		
	Body		
	Features		
Personality			
Good or evil?			
What makes him/her/it different from other creatures?			
Other details			

The Kelpie's Last Battle

2 Now plan a story for your mythical creature to star in.

Country	
Adjectives to describe this country	
Weather	
An event	
A place	
What does the mythical creature do?	
What is the consequence of this?	
What happens at the end of your story?	

FAST FINISHERS
Create an enemy for your mythical creature.

3 Imagine you are a villager who has witnessed the fight between the kelpie and the fairy bull. You are being interviewed by a journalist. Write the interview as a script. Include notes to describe the set, and stage directions to say where characters will stand and how they will move and speak. Be ready to perform your script!

❓ PRACTICE QUESTION
Read the first part of the extract, lines 1 to 16, again.
List four things you learn about the crofter's daughter in these lines. [4 marks]

2 The Odyssey

By Joel Skidmore, adapted from Homer's *Odyssey*

▲ The blinding of the Cyclops by Odysseus

LEARNING OBJECTIVES

- To explain why the writer has made certain language choices (such as narrative approach, emotive language and use of imagery).
- To explain why the writer has made structural choices at both sentence level and whole-text level.
- To see how texts fit into their cultural and historical settings.

CONTEXT

The Odyssey is a Greek epic poem which was said to have been first recited thousands of years ago by a poet called Homer. Homer was a blind poet who never wrote down his poetry. Instead, he would recite it and people would spend time listening to the long narratives. *The Odyssey* tells of the wanderings of Odysseus, who was a Greek fighter in the Trojan War. On his way back from the war, Odysseus annoyed the god of the sea, Poseidon, and was forced to spend ten years away from home, often encountering dangerous and evil creatures. In this extract, Odysseus and his men have been trapped in a cave by a one-eyed Cyclops, whose name is Polyphemus, and Odysseus plans their escape.

Use of first person narrative shows us Odysseus' point of view.

It was up to me to make a plan. I found a tree trunk that the Cyclops intended for a walking stick. We cut off a six-foot section, skinned it, put a sharp point on one end and hardened it in the fire. Then we hid it under a pile of manure.

Skidmore has used listing here to show us that Odysseus and his men are busy making something.

When the Cyclops came home and made his usual meal, I spoke to him. 'Cyclops, you might as well take some of our liquor to savour with your barbarous feast.'

This word shows that the Cyclops is barbaric as he likes eating humans.

Odysseus plans to make the Cyclops drunk.

I'd bought along a skin of wine that we'd been given as a gift. It was so strong that we usually diluted it in water twenty to one. The Cyclops tossed it back and then demanded more.

The verb 'demanded' shows that the Cyclops is not very likeable.

'I like you, Greek,' he said. 'I'm going to do you a favour. What's your name?'

The Odyssey

Annotation	Text	Annotation
Polyphemus wants to eat all of Odysseus' men before he eats Odysseus, which shows what a cruel monster he is.	'My name is Nobody,' I told him.	Odysseus hasn't given the Cyclops his real name because he wants to mislead him.
The simile 'like a battering ram' shows how forcefully they have to push the pole into the Cyclops' eye.	It turned out that the favour he intended was to eat me last. But when the wine had knocked him out, I put my plan into effect. Heating the end of pole until it was glowing red, we ran it toward the Cyclops like a battering ram, aiming it for his eye and driving it deep. The thing sizzled like hot metal dropped in water while I twisted it like an auger.	By twisting the pole into the Cyclops' eye, Odysseus is ensuring that his eye is permanently damaged.
Skidmore says that Odysseus and his men drove the pole 'deep' into the eye of the Cyclops in order to blind him.	Polyphemus came awake with a roar, tore the spike from his eye and began groping for us in his blindness.	
	His screams of frustration and rage brought the neighbouring Cyclopes to the mouth of the cave.	Polyphemus lives on an island with his brothers who come running out of their caves when he begins screaming.
	'What is it, brother?' they called inside. 'Is someone harming you?'	
	'It's Nobody!' bellowed Polyphemus.	Think back to the beginning of the extract. Why do you think Odysseus told Polyphemus that his name was 'Nobody'? What does this reveal about Odysseus' character?
	'Then for the love of Poseidon pipe down in there!'	
	They went away, and Polyphemus heaved the boulder aside and spent the night by the open door, hoping we'd be stupid enough to try to sneak past him. Getting past him was the problem alright, but by morning I'd worked out a solution.	
Odysseus and his men escape by tying themselves underneath the goats.	Tying goats together with ropes of willow, I hid a man under each group of three. When it was time to let them out to pasture, the Cyclops ran his hands over their backs but did not notice the men underneath. Myself, I clutched to the underbelly of the biggest ram.	
	'Why aren't you leading the flock as usual?' asked Polyphemus, detaining this beast at the door and stroking its fleece. 'I wish you could talk, so you could point out those Greeks.'	
	He let the ram go, and we beat it down to the ship as fast as our legs would carry us. When we were a good way out to sea, I could not resist a taunt. I called out, and Polyphemus came to the edge of the seaside cliff. In his fury he tore up a huge boulder and flung it at us.	Odysseus enjoys making fun of the Cyclops and taunts him.
	It landed in front of our bow, and the splash almost drove us back onto the beach. This time I waited until my panicked men had rowed a good bit further before I put my hands to my mouth to call out again. The men tried to hush me, but I was aquiver with triumph.	Odysseus' men try to silence him but he continues mocking the Cyclops, which shows his foolish character.
	'If someone asks who did this, the name is Odysseus!'	
	That brought another boulder hurtling our way, but this one landed astern and only hastened our departure. The Cyclops was left howling on the cliff, calling out to his father Poseidon for vengeance.	Poseidon will now become angry with Odysseus because the Cyclops is his son.

Fiction

▲ A wine skin

GLOSSARY

Barbarous: very cruel
Skin of wine: a leather bag that is used to carry wine
Auger: a tool used for drilling that looks like a large corkscrew

SKILLS FOCUS

✔ Distinguish main ideas in a text.
✔ Choose true and false statements.
✔ Show awareness of how language choices affect meaning.

LOOK CLOSER

1. Read the extract again. What do we learn about the Cyclops in this extract? Think about:
   - his appearance
   - his personality
   - the language that Skidmore uses to describe him.

2. Why does Odysseus tell Polyphemus that his name is Nobody? How does this link to what happens later on in the extract?

3. Skidmore uses lots of figurative language in this extract, such as interesting imagery, similes and metaphors. Find examples of these and discuss the effect of them. You can use the table below to help you.

Type of language, e.g. simile	Quotation	Effect, e.g. This makes the reader feel …

4. How can we tell that the blinding of Polyphemus is gruesome? Write a paragraph, with evidence, explaining your answer.

The Odyssey

NOW TRY THIS

1 Imagine that the Cyclops meets his brothers after he has been blinded. Create a storyboard, with pictures and text, summarising what happens. You can use the structure below to help you.

1) 	2)	3)
Nobody blinded me!		
4)	5)	6)

FAST FINISHERS

- Imagine you are a member of Odysseus' crew. Write a diary entry explaining what you think about his leadership of your group.

2 Imagine that you are the blinded Cyclops, Polyphemus. Prepare a speech to your brothers, explaining what happened to you, why you are upset and what you would like done to Odysseus. Be ready to perform your speech to the rest of the class.

PRACTICE QUESTION

Read the extract again. Choose four statements below which are true.
- Copy out the ones that you think are true.
- Choose a maximum of four true statements. **[4 Marks]**

A Odysseus uses a branch as a weapon. ☐
B The Cyclops is called Polyphemus. ☐
C Odysseus tells the Cyclops his name is Nobody. ☐
D Odysseus offers the Cyclops some wine. ☐
E The Cyclops says he will eat Odysseus first. ☐
F Odysseus doesn't know how to defeat the Cyclops. ☐
G Odysseus blinds the Cyclops. ☐
H The Cyclops dies at the end of the story. ☐

3 King Arthur

Retold by Deborah Tempest

▲ A portrait of King Arthur

LEARNING OBJECTIVES

- To identify and interpret explicit and implicit ideas.
- To comment on how writers use language and techniques to achieve effects.
- To select purposeful evidence in order to support ideas.

CONTEXT

In this extract, we will be exploring one of the most famous stories involving King Arthur: the Sword in the Stone. According to legend, there was a magical sword placed in a large stone in Westminster, London. On the stone was an inscription:

'Whoso pulleth out this sword from this stone, is right wise King born of all England.'

For many years, lots of strong noblemen came from far and wide and attempted to lift the sword from the stone but were unable to. When Arthur was 16 years old, Merlin brought him to the stone. Arthur was easily able to pull the sword from the stone and was crowned King of England. The legend of King Arthur was first mentioned in a book from the twelfth century AD by the writer Geoffrey of Monmouth. We will be reading a more modern version that was written for children.

When Arthur was a young man, Merlin went to London. He visited the Archbishop, the most important man in the Church.

'Call the knights to London. Then we will find the new king,' Merlin told the Archbishop.

The knights came to London. They met at a large church, and the Archbishop spoke to them. When they came outside, they saw something strange in front of the church. It was a very large stone with a huge, glittering sword in it. The sun shone on the sword and it looked very strong. The knights were excited, and started to talk about it.

'Where did it come from?'

'How did it get here?'

'Who brought the stone here? We didn't see anybody. And who put the sword in it?'

> Merlin is a wizard who keeps an eye on Arthur.

> The sun shining on the sword emphasises its importance in the story.

> The writer has used lots of dialogue to show how excited the knights are about the sword in the stone.

King Arthur

On the stone were these words:

> ONLY THE KING CAN TAKE THE SWORD FROM THE STONE.

Every knight tried to pull the sword out of the stone. Nobody could do it — the sword did not come out. The knights pulled and pulled with relentless effort but they could not move the sword.

'Our king is not here,' said the Archbishop. 'But I know that we will find him.'

Ten knights stayed and watched the stone. The Archbishop invited all the great men in the country to London for a huge battle. There were many battles at that time. People fought on horses with swords in their hands. The strongest and best knight always won.

'Perhaps the new king will come to the fight,' thought the Archbishop.

Sir Ector went to the fight with his two sons, Sir Kay and young Arthur. Arthur was now sixteen years old, and had become a brave and handsome man. The young men wanted to fight with the other knights, but Sir Kay did not have a sword. Arthur was a kind young man. He wanted to help.

'There is a sword in a stone outside a church. I saw it on the way here. I will get it and fight with it. Then you can have my sword,' he said to his brother.

Arthur left Sir Kay and quickly went to the church. There were no knights outside by the stone because they were at the fight. Arthur climbed down from his horse and went to the stone. He did not read the words on the stone. He took the sword in his hand and pulled. It came out of the stone effortlessly. Arthur was unaware of the significance of this moment.

He ran back to his horse with the sword. Some minutes later, he met Sir Kay and Sir Ector again, and he showed them the sword.

'Where did that sword come from?' Sir Ector asked, amazed. He knew about the words on the stone.

They went back to the place outside the church, and Sir Ector put the sword in the stone again.

'Now pull it out,' he said to Arthur.

Arthur pulled it out. It came out as easily as a knife out of butter. Sir Ector saw this and took Arthur's hand in awe. 'You are my king,' he said.

Arthur did not understand. What did his father mean? 'Arthur,' Sir Ector said slowly, 'I love you very much, but I am not really your father. Merlin, the famous man of magic, brought you to me when you were a small child. I took you into my family because he asked me. Now I know that you are the king.'

- The knights are desperate to pull the sword from the stone because they want to be king.
- Swords were prestigious weapons that were used by knights in the Middle Ages. Ordinary soldiers did not use them.
- Arthur's offer to his brother shows that he is generous and kind.
- Arthur does not read the words next to the stone, so he has no idea how significant this moment actually is.
- Sir Ector questions Arthur about the sword because he recognises it.
- The simile 'as a knife out of butter' shows how easily Arthur was able to pull the sword from the stone.
- Sir Ector tells Arthur that he is now king because he pulled the sword from the stone. He also tells him that he was adopted.

Fiction

GLOSSARY

Archbishop: the highest ranking bishop who is in charge of other bishops in the church

SKILLS FOCUS

✔ Distinguish main ideas in a text.
✔ Find and list information.
✔ Recognise implicit ideas in a text.

LOOK CLOSER

1. Read the extract again. What do we learn about Arthur in this extract? Think about:
   - his appearance
   - his personality
   - the language that Tempest uses to describe him.

2. Why are all of the knights desperate to pull the sword from the stone?

3. Arthur does not read the writing on the stone before he pulls it out the first time. Why do you think that this is important? What does it reveal about Arthur? Write a paragraph explaining your views.

4. What qualities does Arthur possess that show that he will make a good king? Write a paragraph, with evidence, explaining your answer.

King Arthur

NOW TRY THIS

1 Imagine that you are a newspaper reporter who witnessed the events in London when Arthur removed the sword from the stone. Write a report for the newspaper explaining what happened. Make sure that you use the 5Ws in your report:

- **What** happened?
- **Where** did it happen?
- **When** did it happen?
- **Who** was involved?
- **Why** did it happen?

Try to write three paragraphs and include speech and eyewitness accounts.

FAST FINISHERS

- Write a description of Merlin. Consider his appearance and personality.
- Write Arthur's diary entry after he removes the sword from the stone. Make sure that you write in the first person narrative, as Arthur, describing what happened to you and the consequences of your actions.

You could begin your diary like this.

> Dear Diary
> I can hardly believe what happened today ...

2 Write the script for a TV news report where you interview both Arthur and Merlin about the removal of the sword from the stone. Include notes to describe the set, and stage directions to say where characters will stand and how they will move and speak. Be ready to perform your script!

PRACTICE QUESTION

Read the first part of the extract, lines 6 to 12, again.
List four things you learn about the sword in the stone in these lines. [4 marks]

4 Hercules

Retold by Lilian Stoughton Hyde

▲ Hercules wrestling a lion

LEARNING OBJECTIVES

- To identify and interpret explicit and implicit ideas.
- To recognise writers' techniques, such as adjectives, emotive language and imagery.
- To comment on the writer's presentation of characters.

CONTEXT

The Ancient Greek stories of Hercules are about a young man, Hercules, and the 12 labours that he has to endure. Hercules is the younger cousin of King Eurystheus, and this means that he is destined to be his slave. King Eurystheus is extremely jealous of his strong cousin, Hercules, and makes him fulfil 12 increasingly difficult labours. For his first labour, Hercules has to wrestle a lion.

The stories of Hercules date back to the Etruscan era, which was from 700BC to AD50. They were passed from generation to generation by word of mouth before being written down.

Eurystheus thought it would be an excellent plan to send Hercules to kill the Nemean lion. So he assigned this for his cousin's first task.

Eurystheus doesn't want Hercules to succeed in his labours so gives him challenging tasks.

Without having any very definite idea of how he was to accomplish this task, the young hero took his bow and arrows and started out. At the foot of Mount Helicon he found a wild olive tree, one that had grown slowly in stony soil, and was tough of fibre and full of knots. Instead of lopping off a branch for his purpose, as a weaker man might have done, Hercules pulled up this whole tree by the roots, and made a stout club of it. Then he went to the Nemean valley.

Hyde uses the phrase 'young hero' to show that Hercules is already brave.

Hercules is able to pull an entire tree from its roots, which shows how powerful he is.

Not a herdsman nor a shepherd was in sight for whom he could inquire about the beast; for they were all afraid of it, and kept within doors, leaving their flocks to its mercy.

The villagers are scared to go outside because of the lion.

18

Hercules

Hercules watched, near the temple, all day long. Toward night, the lion came home to its lair. It looked very fierce and terrible. Its mane was all dashed with blood, and it was licking fresh blood from its chin. Hiding himself among some bushes, Hercules fixed an arrow into his bow. When the lion came near enough, he sent the arrow, singing, straight to its flank, but it glanced away, and fell on the grass. The lion paused in its slow walk, looked to the right and the left, and showed its teeth. Then Hercules shot another arrow, but this one glanced away like the first; for this was no common lion, and its skin was very tough. Hercules was making ready to shoot a third time, when the lion saw him. It lashed its tail, then crouched and sprang. Hercules met it with his club, and broke the club on its head, but stunned it in doing so. Then he seized its neck with both hands, and succeeded in strangling it, as he had strangled the snakes, when he was only a baby, in his shield cradle. So ended the first of the twelve labours of Hercules.

When Hercules went back to King Eurystheus, he wore the skin of the Nemean lion over his shoulders, with the head of the beast resting on his own head like a kind of helmet. Eurystheus would hardly have been more frightened if he had suddenly seen the Nemean lion itself walking into his palace.

Hercules soon made himself another club, and after this he was seldom seen without both his club and his lion's skin.

Annotations (left):
- Hyde has used blood imagery here to describe the lion and how ferocious it is.
- Hyde uses three verbs here to describe what the lion does: lashed, crouched and sprang.
- Hercules strangles the lion with his bare hands, showing us his immense strength.
- Hercules wears the skin of the lion, showing how he has defeated it.
- The club and lion's skin become Hercules' costume and show the world how brave and strong he is.

Annotations (right):
- The verb 'singing' shows the noise the arrow makes when it goes flying through the air.
- The lion has very tough skin which means an arrow cannot pierce through and kill it.
- King Eurystheus is frightened by Hercules because nobody has defeated the lion before.

GLOSSARY

Nemean lion: a fierce lion found in Greece that was difficult to kill
Lopping off: cutting off a branch
Stout club: a strong and thick stick used as a weapon
Herdsman: a man who looks after a large group of animals
Labours: difficult challenges

SKILLS FOCUS

- ✔ Recognise implicit ideas in a text.
- ✔ Recognise writers' techniques.
- ✔ Comment on writers' presentation of characters, using appropriate references from the text.

Fiction

LOOK CLOSER

1. Read Paragraph 2 again. What do we learn about Hercules in this extract? Think about:
   - his appearance
   - his personality
   - the language that Hyde uses to describe him.

2. Who is Hercules' cousin? Why do you think that this person hates Hercules so much?

3. The villagers are extremely scared of the lion. How can you tell? Make sure that you use quotations in your answer.

4. Read Paragraph 4 again. How does Hyde use gruesome language to describe the lion? Write a paragraph, with evidence, explaining your answer.

NOW TRY THIS

1. Write a fact file about Hercules. You can use the table below to help you.

Fact file		
Name		Hercules
Appearance	Face	
	Body	
	Features	
Personality		
Good or evil?		
What makes him different from other heroes?		
Other details		

FAST FINISHERS
Write a description of another labour that you think Hercules could face.

Hercules

2 Now write a fact file about the lion, using the table below to help you.

Fact file		
Name		Nemean lion
Appearance	Face	
	Body	
	Features	
Personality		
Good or evil?		
What makes him different from other lions?		
Other details		

FAST FINISHERS
Write a description of Hercules. Consider his appearance and personality.

3 Imagine Hercules meets his cousin, King Eurystheus, for the first time. The King tells Hercules that he is his slave and has to perform 12 tasks, or labours, for him. In pairs, write the script for this meeting. Once you have done this, practise reading your script before performing it to the rest of the class.

❓ PRACTICE QUESTION

Read the extract again. How does Hyde use language to show the reader that Hercules is strong? Write at least three paragraphs in response.
Here are some sentence starters to help you with your first paragraph:

- The first way that Hyde uses language to show us that Hercules is strong is …
- In the extract Hyde writes …
- This suggests that … [8 marks]

5 The Ruin of Pennard Castle

By Graham Watkins

▲ The ruins of Pennard Castle

LEARNING OBJECTIVES

- To distinguish main ideas and select relevant points in texts.
- To consider the writer's presentation of characters.
- To see how texts fit into their cultural and historical settings.

CONTEXT

Pennard Castle in Wales has been abandoned since the 1400s. There are many theories about why it was abandoned, one of the most scientific being that the build up of sand meant that the castle was uninhabitable. However, one myth that has been passed down from one generation to the next by the people of Pennard is that fairies cursed the baron who lived in the castle, as he did not welcome them to his wedding feast. The fairies then caused a sandstorm which destroyed the castle.

In ancient times when the strong took what they wanted with a sword and the weak hid in terror, there was a Baron so fierce and ruthless that everyone feared him. His strength and bravery in battle was known throughout Wales and women scolded their children by whispering his name. Even his own men at arms cowered when he looked at them and his enemies never dared venture near his castle on the remote peninsular called 'Gower'. It was here that he passed his time in debauchery and drunkenness.

War was in the land and, fearing defeat, the King of Gwynedd, Lord of Snowdonia, sent a message to the Baron pleading for help. Eager for a fight, but shrewd enough to see an opportunity for profit, the Baron sent a messenger back to the King demanding to know what his reward would be. The King was desperate. His enemies were collecting a large army in the east and he knew that his throne would soon be lost. The messenger quickly returned to the Baron's castle.

'Well,' bellowed the Baron. 'What does your lord and master offer that I may take his side in this matter?'

'My master commands that I give you this,' he replied, handing the Baron a scroll with a royal seal. It was the King's guarantee to reward the Baron with anything he desired if they won the battle. The Baron tucked the scroll inside his shirt and called his men to arms. They rode swiftly to the north and joined the King. The army of Gwynedd was small and outnumbered many times over. Some were ready to turn and run but not the Baron. He charged straight at the enemy,

---

Annotations:

- The Baron is so frightening that parents can scare their children by mentioning him.
- The Baron lives in 'debauchery' and 'drunkenness' which shows how unpleasant he is.
- The Baron will only help the King if he is given a prize, showing his selfishness.
- The Baron 'bellowed', showing he is a loud person.
- The King comes across quite differently from the Baron here, being someone who is sensible and respected.
- Watkins uses the violent verbs 'hacking' and 'slashing' to emphasise the violence of the Baron's movements.

The Ruin of Pennard Castle

hacking and slashing with his sword. No one could stand against his strength. As he cut and thrust, men fell right and left leaving a swathe through the ranks like a scythe through corn. The Baron's charge continued until he reached the battle flags of the invaders. Here stood the dukes and princes that led the invading army. The Baron cut them down, seized the flags and threw them to the ground.

Seeing their leaders slain, the attackers turned and fled. The battle was won. The victors rode to Caernarfon Castle and there were great celebrations. The King was determined to reward his mighty warrior.

'What prize shall you have?' he asked the Baron, ready to empty his treasury. 'Name it and it is yours.'

'You have a beautiful daughter, Sire. She will be my reward,' answered the Baron. The King was dismayed. This was not the bargain he expected but he had given his word and a king's word is not broken lightly.

The King's daughter was beautiful but she was also a bit impressionable. She was certainly lonely and seldom had visitors. Some claimed that her friends were fairies and that she spent her days talking to them. The Baron's demand flattered her. This hulk of a man was a mighty warrior and she liked the idea that he wanted her. Despite being a little afraid, the Princess agreed to wed the Baron. With a sad heart, the King bade her farewell.

As they journeyed south to Pennard Castle, the Baron boasted about his bravery and strength. As he bragged, her thoughts slowly turned from flattery and curiosity to doubt. She realised the Baron was a brute and wondered if she had done the right thing. Reaching Pennard Castle, the Baron ordered a great feast. The feasting soon turned to drunkenness.

Suddenly, there was a cry from the guards.

'An army comes to Pennard.' The Baron ran to the battlements and saw a horde carrying lanterns, advancing toward his Castle. He grabbed his sword and ran out to meet the attackers. He cut right and left, slashing and swinging as he ran through the invaders. The lights swarmed around him and he drove on, hacking and chopping. As he fought, his sword grew heavy and his arms burned with pain from the exertion, until he could fight no more.

The Baron slumped to his knees, exhausted. His sword slid from his weary hands. Sober now, he looked up at the twinkling lights dancing around him and imagined he saw the faint glimmer of gossamer wings. This was no army, but a host of fairies coming to share in the wedding celebrations.

As he watched, the wind blew the fairies away and a violent storm started to batter the Castle. The same night a mountain of sand blew in from the sea. The Castle, the Baron and the Princess vanished. The ruin that you see today is all that is left from that fateful night.

Annotations (left side):
- The Baron throws the flags to the ground to show that he has defeated the enemy.
- The King is ready to 'empty his treasury' and give money to the Baron.
- The King's daughter is quite an innocent creature who believes in fairies and sees the good in people.
- The Princess realises that the Baron is not a nice man.
- The Baron is usually strong in battle but this battle is different as he has become very tired and can no longer fight.

Annotations (right side):
- The Baron cuts through the men 'like a scythe through corn'. This simile suggests that he is ruthless in battle and kills many people.
- Again, the King is seen in a much more positive way than the Baron, keeping his promise.
- The King is upset because the Baron wants his daughter as a 'prize'.
- The Princess is flattered by the attention that the Baron gives her.
- The Baron assumes that the people coming towards the castle want to have a fight.
- Watkins uses verbs here to show how violent the Baron is.
- The Baron realises that he has been fighting fairies, not soldiers.

23

Fiction

SKILLS FOCUS

- ✔ Distinguish main ideas and select relevant points from the texts.
- ✔ Recognise explicit and implicit ideas.
- ✔ Comment on the writer's presentation of character.
- ✔ Show awareness of how language choices affect meaning.

GLOSSARY

Cowered: crouch down in fear
Peninsular: an area of land almost surrounded by water
Debauchery: drinking and being immoral
Gwynedd: a county in Wales
Snowdonia: a region in North-West Wales that has lots of mountains
Shrewd: being clever and sharp
Royal seal: a piece of wax with a design on it that is used to seal an envelope or letter
Swathe: a fallen row of dead soldiers
Scythe: a tool for cutting crops such as corn
Slain: killed
Caernarfon Castle: a large castle in Wales
Horde: a large group of people
Gossamer: a light and thin substance

LOOK CLOSER

1. Read the first paragraph again. Explain how the Baron is presented here. Think about:
   - his appearance
   - his personality
   - the language that Watkins uses to describe him.

2. Even though the Baron is a horrible man, why does the King ask him for help? Give three reasons.

3. Read Paragraph 4 again. How does Watkins use language to describe the Baron? Fill in the table below:

Language feature	Example	Effect
Verbs		These make the reader feel …
Simile		
Metaphor		

4. Explain why the Princess wanted to marry the Baron. Support your answer with reference to the text.

The Ruin of Pennard Castle

NOW TRY THIS

1 Imagine that you are the princess. Write a diary entry from the night before she marries the Baron. Why does she decide to get married? Make sure you write in first person narrative. Write at least three paragraphs.

FAST FINISHERS
Write a description of the Baron. Consider his appearance and personality.

2 Imagine that you work for the Welsh Tourist Board. Design a leaflet encouraging people to visit Pennard Castle. Make sure that you include the following in your leaflet
- Facts about the castle, including its location
- A picture
- A map
- Information about the myth of the castle.

3 Imagine you witness the final battle between the Baron and the fairies. Write an eyewitness account of what you saw. Once you have done this, share your eyewitness account with the rest of the class.

? PRACTICE QUESTION

Read the story again. How does Watkins use verbs throughout the story to show us how violent the Baron is? Write at least three paragraphs in response. Here are some sentence starters to help you with your first paragraph:
- Watkins uses verbs to show us that ...
- In the extract Watkins writes ...
- This suggests that ...   [8 marks]

6 Pan Gu and the Creation of the World

Retold by Shelley Fu

▲ Pan Gu creating the Earth

LEARNING OBJECTIVES
- To show awareness of the main ideas and themes in the text.
- To consider the methods that the writer has used in order to convey these themes.
- To see how texts fit into their cultural and historical settings.

CONTEXT
In many versions of Chinese mythology, Pan Gu is seen as the first living being and the creator of the world. In the story below, we will learn how Pan Gu was born and how he created the Earth. The story of Pan Gu is very old, originating from the Western Zu dynasty which lasted from 1046BC to 221BC.

The Chinese believe that in the beginning, the universe was empty except for a big ball of energy shaped like a chicken egg. This ball of energy had existed since the beginning of time and was called Chaos. Inside the egg, only mist swirled about until, one day, the first living creature formed in Chaos.

The Chinese believed that everything in the universe came from chaos, which was in the shape of an egg.

His name is Pan Gu, and he is the ancestor of us all. After he was formed, he slept for a long time while his body grew bigger and bigger. At first, his body was very small. But after 18,000 years, he grew so extremely big that Chaos could no longer hold him. His strong and heavy head poked against one end of Chaos, and his sturdy feet strained against the other end.

Fu uses adjectives such as 'heavy' and 'sturdy' to show us that Pan Gu is strong.

By this time, Pan Gu was enormous beyond measure. In the small and narrow space of Chaos, Pan Gu was cramped and uncomfortable. One day, he became so uncomfortable that he awoke. He opened his eyes in amazement. Beyond the haziness of Chaos, Pan Gu saw darkness so inky that nothing else was visible.

'Inky' darkness means that it was pitch black.

'I'll soon change this situation,' thought Pan Gu to himself. He stretched out his hand and made an immense fist, which he struck against the wall of Chaos with all his might. Ka-bam! The shell of the egg of Chaos cracked.

'Ka-bam!' shows the movement of Pan Gu's fist.

Pan Gu and the Creation of the World

Juxtaposition, or contrast, is used here to show the difference between the sky and the Earth.

As the stuff of Chaos leaked out into the darkness, the clear and light energy, called the Yang by the Chinese, curled upwards and formed the beautiful blue sky. The heavier, **murkier** elements, called the Yin, sank to form the earth. After Chaos was divided, the universe became a bright wide space. But the distance between sky and earth was very small, and the elements of sky and earth would frequently mix. Pan Gu couldn't stand up straight between this space and felt like dividing the two so that more distance separated them.

Pan Gu wants a bigger divide between Earth and heaven because he can't stand up straight.

Finally, one day, Pan Gu was so bothered that he planted his huge feet on the ground and his hands against the sky. Pan Gu grew an inch every day, and the sky was accordingly pushed one inch higher each day and the earth grew one inch thicker from the pressure of his heavy weight. Time passed. Day after day, Pan Gu stood between heaven and earth, not daring to let go of his hold on the sky, afraid that heaven and earth would mix and all would revert to Chaos.

Pan Gu doesn't want Earth and heaven to mix more because it will cause chaos.

The repetition of the 'S' sound mirrors the sound of the seas and oceans.

His salty sweat streamed down from his forehead, stinging his eyes, but he couldn't mop it away. It flowed down his body and fell as rain and **dew** onto the ground, where it collected into pools to form the seas and the oceans.

Pan Gu finds it hard to support the sky and makes sounds as a result.

The work of supporting the sky was extremely hard, and Pan Gu could not suppress a deep sigh of suffering. His breath turned into the floating clouds and the wind, and the sound of his sigh became the rumbling thunder. Over many, many years, he saw the heavens slowly rise and the earth grow thicker and thicker, and he rejoiced. Finally, after another 18,000 years, the sky was very high and the earth very thick. There was no longer any danger of sky and earth mixing. At last, Pan Gu was satisfied and let go his hold. But the **strenuous** work of holding earth and sky apart for so long had exhausted Pan Gu, and he fell to the ground immediately.

Pan Gu is finally satisfied with his creation.

His body became the massive mountains, his blood and body fluids the surging rivers. His **sinews** and veins transformed into narrow and crooked roads, his skin and muscles the fertile fields. The hairs on his skin turned into the beautiful and **multitudinous** grass, flowers, trees, and woods. Even his bones and teeth turned into bright, hard gold, brilliant jewels, and precious pearls. His beautiful hair flew up and filled the whole sky with countless bright stars.

Lots of adjectives are used here which link to the theme of nature and show the reader how beautiful the Earth is.

Pan Gu was still not dead and observed the changes with great satisfaction. He knew he was dying, but he wanted to gaze upon his work for ever. He winked and sent his left eye into the clear sky, where it turned into the golden sun. He winked again, and his right eye also sailed past the clouds and turned into the bright and silvery moon. Thus, to this day, Pan Gu looks lovingly down upon his greatest creation, the **bountiful** and beautiful earth.

Pan Gu's eyes become the Sun and the Moon.

Fiction

GLOSSARY

Murkier: darker and gloomier
Dew: drops of water
Strenuous: difficult
Sinews: tissues that join muscles to bones
Multitudinous: numerous
Bountiful: plentiful

SKILLS FOCUS

✔ Show awareness of the main ideas and themes of texts.
✔ Recognise some of the methods used to convey these ideas and themes.
✔ Use appropriate references to support points.

LOOK CLOSER

1. Read the first three paragraphs again. How is Pan Gu presented here? Think about:
   - his appearance
   - his personality
   - the language that Fu uses to describe him.

2. What are Yin and Yang, and why does Pan Gu want to separate them?

3. Read Paragraph 9 again. How does Fu use adjectives to show us how beautiful the Earth is? Copy and complete the table below:

Adjective	Effect
	This makes the reader feel ...

4. Now write a step-by-step list of how Pan Gu created the Earth. You could start like this:
   - Pan Gu was formed out of a ball of energy called Chaos.
   - He used his fist to break out of the ball of Chaos.

5. How is the theme of nature presented in this extract? Think about the language that Fu uses to describe nature.

Pan Gu and the Creation of the World

NOW TRY THIS

1. Imagine that you are Pan Gu. Write a description of how you created the Earth to share with others. Make sure you write in first person narrative. Write at least three paragraphs.

FAST FINISHERS
Write a description of the Earth after it has been created by Pan Gu. Use lots of adjectives in your description.

2. Imagine that you are a primary school teacher. Write a poster or comic strip for Year 1 children describing the Pan Gu story. Make sure that you include the following in your poster:
   - a step-by-step account of how the Earth was formed
   - vocabulary that Year 1 children will understand
   - bright illustrations.

3. There are many different creation myths. Think about your own background, culture or religion. Is there a special story about the way that the Earth was created? Write down a summary of a creation story that you know and then retell it to a partner.

PRACTICE QUESTION

Read the story of how Pan Gu created the world again. How has Fu used language to interest you as a reader? Write three paragraphs. Here are some sentence starters to help you:

- **Paragraph 1**
  At the start of the story, Fu uses …
  The text says …
  This interests the reader because …
- **Paragraph 2**
  In the middle of the story, Fu uses …
  She writes …
  This interests the reader because …
- **Paragraph 3**
  Finally, at the end of the story, Fu uses …
  Fu writes …
  This is interesting because …

[8 marks]

7 King Midas and the Golden Touch

By Lilian Stoughton Hyde

▲ King Midas painting by Simon Floquet

LEARNING OBJECTIVES

- To identify and interpret explicit and implicit ideas.
- To make inferences based on evidence.
- To show awareness of how language choices affect meaning.

CONTEXT

The myth of Midas dates back to Ancient Greek times. Aristotle, a Greek philosopher, mentions him in his writing. According to Greek myth, King Midas was a very kind man. He rescued Silenus, an elderly **satyr** who was lost and wandering helplessly in Midas' **vineyards**. King Midas took Silenus back to Bacchus, who was the god of **agriculture** and wine. Bacchus was so grateful that he said he would give King Midas anything he wanted. Midas decided that he would like anything he touched to be turned into gold.

When Bacchus offered him anything that he might ask for, King Midas's first thought was of his **treasury**, and he asked that whatever he touched might be turned into gold. His wish was granted.

King Midas was hardly able to believe in his good fortune. He thought himself the luckiest of men. ◀ ······ King Midas initially feels very happy that his wish has been granted.

At the time his wish was granted he happened to stand under an oak tree, and the first thing he did was to raise his hand and touch one of its branches. Immediately, the branch became the **richest** gold, with all the little acorns as **perfect** as ever. He laughed triumphantly at that, and then he touched a **small** stone, which lay on the ground. This became a **solid** gold **nugget**. Then he picked an apple from a tree, and held a **beautiful, bright, gold** apple in his hand. Oh, there was no doubt about it. King Midas really had the Golden Touch! He thought it too good to be true. After this, he touched the lilies that bordered the walk. They turned from pure white to bright yellow, but **bent their heads lower than ever, as if they were ashamed** of the change that the touch of King Midas had wrought in them.

Hyde uses lots of adjectives here to show us how beautiful things are when they turn into gold. ······▶

Hyde uses personification here: the lilies 'bent their heads lower than ever'. The lilies seem ashamed of King Midas because he is so greedy. ······▶

King Midas and the Golden Touch

Before turning any more things into gold, the king sat down at the little table which his slaves had brought into the court. The parched corn was fresh and crisp, and the grapes juicy and sweet. But when he tasted a grape from one of the luscious clusters, it became a hard ball of gold in his mouth. This was very unpleasant. He laid the gold ball on the table and tried the parched wheat, but only to have his mouth filled with hard yellow metal. Feeling as if he were choking, he took a sip of water, and at the touch of his lips, even this became liquid gold.

Then all his bright treasures began to look ugly to him, and his heart grew as heavy as if that, too, were turning into gold.

That night King Midas lay down under a gorgeous golden counterpane, with his head upon a pillow of solid gold; but he could not rest; sleep would not come to him. As he lay there, he began to fear that his queen, his little children, and all his king friends, might be changed to hard, golden statues.

This would be more deplorable than anything else that had resulted from his foolish wish. Poor Midas saw now that riches were not the most desirable of all things. He was cured forever of his love of gold. The instant it was daylight he rushed to Bacchus, and implored the god to take back his fatal gift.

'Ah,' said Bacchus, smiling, 'so you have gold enough at last. Very well. If you are sure that you do not wish to change anything more into that metal, go and bathe in the spring where the river Pactolus rises. The pure water of that spring will wash away the Golden Touch.'

King Midas gladly obeyed, and became as free from the Golden Touch as when he was a boy watching the ants. But the strange magic was imparted to the waters of the spring, and to this day the river Pactolus has golden sands.

Side notes:
- King Midas is starting to realise some of the disadvantages of his wish.
- Hyde still uses adjectives here but in a far more negative way.
- King Midas' treasures now look unpleasant to him.
- King Midas realises that he is gaining wealth but losing his family and friends.
- Hyde writes that Midas' wish is foolish.
- King Midas begs to give back his wish because it is making him suffer.
- Bacchus is smiling when Midas asks to return the wish, as if he always knew what harm it would cause.
- Midas feels free when he no longer has his wish.

GLOSSARY

Satyr: a woodland god that is half goat and half man
Vineyard: fields of grapevines that are used to make wine
Agriculture: farming
Treasury: a building where money and treasure is stored
Nugget: a small lump of gold or other precious metal
Parched: lightly roasted
Counterpane: bedspread
Deplorable: disgraceful
Implored: begged

Fiction

> **SKILLS FOCUS**
> ✔ Show awareness of the main ideas and themes of texts.
> ✔ Recognise some of the methods used to convey these ideas and themes.
> ✔ Use appropriate references.

LOOK CLOSER

1 Read the extract again. How does King Midas feel about his wealth and how does this change as the extract develops? Fill in the table below:

Point	Evidence	Explanation
At the start of the story, Midas feels ...	Hyde writes ...	This suggests ...
In the middle of the story, Midas ...		
At the end of the story, Midas ...		

2 Now, using your table as a plan, write three paragraphs answering the following question: How does King Midas feel about his wealth and how does this change as the extract develops?

3 Read Paragraphs 2 and 3 again. How does Hyde use adjectives in these paragraphs? Fill in the table below:

Adjective	Effect
	This makes the reader feel ...

4 What do you think the moral of this tale is? How can you tell?

FAST FINISHERS
Can you think of any other tales that have a moral at the end?

King Midas and the Golden Touch

NOW TRY THIS

1 If you could be granted one wish in the world, what would it be and why? Write a short account of a time when your wish comes true!

FAST FINISHERS

Write a lively description of King Midas. Use lots of adjectives and detail in order to bring your writing to life.

2 Get into groups of three. Each group member should pick one of the statements below and discuss this point of view:
- The story of King Midas is about being careful what you wish for.
- The story of King Midas tells us that if you become too rich you forget what is important.
- It is King Midas' personality, not his wealth, that causes his problems.

Spend about five minutes discussing your point of view. At the end of the discussion, decide whose point of view is the most convincing.

PRACTICE QUESTION

Read the story again. How has Hyde made us feel sympathetic towards Midas? Think about what happens to him at the beginning of the story, how this changes in the middle, and then what happens at the end. Write three paragraphs. Here are some sentence starters to help you:

- **Paragraph 1**
  At the start of the story, ...
  The text says ...
  This makes the reader feel ...
- **Paragraph 2**
  In the middle of the story, Hyde ...
  She writes ...
  This makes us feel sorry for Midas because ...
- **Paragraph 3**
  Finally, at the end of the story, ...
  Hyde writes ...
  This makes us feel sympathy because ... [8 marks]

8 Echo
By Lilian Stoughton Hyde

▲ Echo

LEARNING OBJECTIVES
- To recognise writers' techniques, including the use of figurative language.
- To comment on the writers' presentation of characters, using appropriate references from texts.
- To link texts to their social and historical contexts.

CONTEXT
In Ancient Greek mythology, Echo was a nymph. She is first mentioned by the writer Ovid in his book *Metamorphoses*. Echo spoke too much and was rude to Juno, who was Queen of the Gods. As a punishment, Juno made it difficult for Echo to speak. All that Echo could do was repeat the final words of others. Eventually, Echo disappeared altogether, although her sad voice still remained. The moral of the story of Echo is that you should allow others to speak, and you shouldn't be rude.

Echo

Echo was a nymph who talked too much. She was very fond of having the last word. One day she spoke rudely to the great Juno, who said that for this offence Echo should never use her voice again, unless to repeat what she had just heard …

Echo annoyed Juno so much that Juno punished her.

This was almost as bad as if Juno had changed her into a parrot. Echo was very much ashamed, and hid herself in the forest.

Narcissus, a young man who had hair as yellow as gold and eyes as blue as the sky – a very rare thing in Greece, where most people were very dark – used to hunt in the forest where Echo was hiding. As she was peeping out shyly from some cave or from behind a great tree, Echo often saw Narcissus, and she admired him very much.

Similes have been used here to show how fair Narcissus is. In Ancient Greece, you were seen as more beautiful if you had blond hair.

Echo is beginning to fall in love with Narcissus.

Echo

One day Narcissus became separated from his friends, and hearing something rustle among his leaves, he called, 'Who's here?'

'Here,' answered Echo.

'Here I am. Come!' said Narcissus.

'I am come,' said Echo; and as she spoke, she came out from among the trees.

When Narcissus saw a stranger, instead of one of his friends as he had expected, he looked surprised and walked quickly away.

After this, Echo never came out and allowed herself to be seen again, and in time she faded away till she became only a voice.

This voice was heard for many, many years in forests and among mountains, particularly in caves. In their solitary walks, hunters often heard it. Sometimes it mocked the barking of their dogs; sometimes it repeated their own last words. It always had a weird and mournful sound, and seemed to make lonely places more lonely still.

- Echo is hiding in the leaves.
- Narcissus wanted to see his friends, so walked away.
- Echo is so sad that she fades away, turning from a physical presence to just a voice, or an 'echo'.
- Hyde uses lots of emotive language here, such as 'solitary', 'mournful' and 'lonely' which gives a sad tone to the end of the story.

GLOSSARY

Nymph: a mythological spirit
Juno: Queen of the Gods
Solitary: alone, lonely
Mournful: sad

SKILLS FOCUS

✔ Learn about the character of Echo.
✔ Consider the language techniques that Hyde has used.
✔ Consider the moral of the story of Echo.

▲ Narcissus

Fiction

LOOK CLOSER

1. Read the first paragraph again. Explain how Echo is presented here. Think about:
   - her appearance
   - her personality
   - the language that Hyde uses to describe her.

2. Why does Juno punish Echo? What is the punishment that she gives her? Here are some sentence starters to help you:
   - Juno punishes Echo because …
   - The punishment that Juno gives Echo is …

3. Read Paragraph 2 again. How does Hyde use language to describe Echo and Narcissus? Fill in the table below:

Example	Language Feature	Effect
'hair as yellow as gold'		This will make the reader feel …
'eyes as blue as the sky'		
'peeping out shyly'		
'admired him very much'		

FAST FINISHERS

Why do you think that the story ends so sadly? Support your answer with reference to the text. Here are some sentence starters to help you:
- I think that the story ends sadly because …
- In the text, Hyde writes …

Echo

NOW TRY THIS

1 Imagine that you are Juno. Write a diary entry explaining why Echo makes you so angry and why you feel that you must punish her. Make sure that you write using first person narrative. Write at least three paragraphs. You can start like this if you wish:

> Dear Diary
>
> Echo has been so annoying today! She is always talking!

FAST FINISHERS
Write a description of Narcissus. Consider his appearance and personality.

2 Imagine that you are Echo. Write a letter to Juno begging her to give you your voice back. Make sure you include the following:
- first person narrative
- emotive and persuasive language
- your reasons for needing your voice back.

You could start your letter like this:

> Dear Juno,
>
> It has now been a year since you took my voice away from me …

3 Write a play script recreating the meeting between Echo and Narcissus. Remember to include:
- Echo's first glimpse of Narcissus
- Narcissus' rejection of Echo
- Echo's sadness at being rejected.

In pairs, perform your play to the rest of the class.

PRACTICE QUESTION

Reread the second half of the story. How does Hyde use language to make the ending of this story sad? Write at least three paragraphs in response. Here are some sentence starters to help you with your first paragraph:
- Hyde uses emotive language to show us that …
- In the extract, Hyde writes …
- This suggests that …   [8 marks]

Section 2: Non-fiction

9 The Giant's Causeway
From an article on http://ireland.com

LEARNING OBJECTIVES
- To distinguish the main ideas in a text.
- To be able to retrieve implicit and explicit information.
- To analyse the writer's use of language.

CONTEXT
The Giant's Causeway in Northern Ireland is a series of hexagonal shaped stones which are connected to each other, forming a **peninsula**. Scientists believe that the stones are shaped and connected in this peculiar way because of an ancient volcanic eruption. However, many local people believe the legend of Finn McCool. Finn McCool was a giant who had a fight with another giant called Benandonner. Finn threw rocks into the sea to encourage Benandonner to come to him so that they could fight. It was these hexagonal rocks that formed the Giant's Causeway. The article below, which is from a website, explores the history of the Giant's Causeway.

▲ The Giant's Causeway

The giant story

Antrim's Giant's Causeway is a 60-million-year-old story of science. Or is it?

CNN's John D Sutter is touring the island of Ireland clockwise. Eventually, he arrives to what he calls 'Northern Ireland's most popular attraction'.

His description of the Giant's Causeway hints at the magical: 'A golf-course green canyon wall slopes into a set of volcanic rock formations that are completely surreal: Near-perfect hexagon tubes are stacked next to each other like puzzle pieces.'

Something this pretty couldn't be the result of a volcanic eruption 60 million years ago, could it?

Well, there are two lines of thought on that one. The first involves a certain giant by the name of Finn McCool (also known as Fionn mac Cumhaill).

The writer has used a rhetorical question here to make the reader curious.

The stones are described as 'surreal' because they have created this amazing formation.

The rhetorical question has been used here to suggest that the stones are so pretty that the pattern couldn't have been created by chance.

The adjectives 'most popular' show how many people want to see the Giant's Causeway.

'Golf-course green' suggests that the green is the colour of grass.

The writer has used the simile 'like puzzle pieces' to show how complex the stones are and how they have been cleverly put together.

The Giant's Causeway

Giant fights

Finn is having trouble with someone across the water. The Scottish giant Benandonner is threatening Ireland. An enraged Finn grabs chunks of the Antrim coast and throws them into the sea. The rock forms a path for Finn to follow and teach Benandonner a lesson.

Bad idea – Benandonner is terrifyingly massive. Finn beats a hasty retreat, followed by the giant, only to be saved by our hero's quick-thinking wife who disguised him as a baby. The angry Scot saw the baby and decided if the child was that big, the daddy must be really huge.

Mythical landscapes, magical tales

For Eleanor Killough from the National Trust, the Finn story holds water: 'Of course it was Finn McCool! That's what we the locals believe anyway.'

'We give our visitors the two sides of the coin – the stories and the science and let them decide, but most visitors leave believing this place is an ancient home of a mighty giant.'

As Eleanor says, though, there are two sides to the story.

The science bit

'The Giant's Causeway is the aftermath of volcanic crashing, burning and cooling,' Eleanor explains. 'An epic, 60-million-year-old legacy to lava. Over 40,000 basalt columns: interlocked.'

'It's no wonder this place is a UNESCO World Heritage Site because beyond the mindboggling beauty, the Causeway is our portal into Earth's most ancient past,' she concludes.

Picture-perfect scenes

Whatever you choose to believe, there's no disputing that the Causeway makes a pretty picture – thousands of tourists click their cameras here every year.

Giant or science? Maybe you should check it out for yourself.

Annotations:

- Finn has been described as 'enraged' to show how angry he is.
- The Scot thinks that Finn is just a baby. He gets really scared as he wonders how big the baby's parents would be.
- 'Two sides of the coin' is a metaphor to show that visitors are given the myth and the scientific facts.
- The writer has used lots of statistics here to show how old the stones are.
- The stones are so unique that they have been described as 'mindboggling'.
- The writer has used juxtaposition here to show the contrast between science and legend.

Non-fiction

GLOSSARY

Peninsula: an area of land that juts out and is almost entirely surrounded by water
Antrim: a county in Northern Ireland
CNN: an American news channel
Clockwise: the direction that the hands on a clock go in
Surreal: strange
Hasty retreat: leaving very quickly
National Trust: a charity that helps to protect and look after important landmarks and buildings in Great Britain
Holds water: an expression that suggests that an argument could be true
UNESCO World Heritage Site: a landmark, building or piece of land that is considered of considerable importance and is protected by UNESCO, an international conservation agency
Portal: a doorway

▲ 'A golf-course green canyon wall'

SKILLS FOCUS

✔ Explore how the writer uses language techniques to convey ideas.
✔ Choose true and false statements.

LOOK CLOSER

1 Have a look at this section of the text:

> A golf-course green canyon wall slopes into a set of volcanic rock formations that are completely surreal: Near-perfect hexagon tubes are stacked next to each other like puzzle pieces.

How has the writer made the Giant's Causeway seem magical? Think about the use of:

- adjectives
- the word 'surreal'
- similes.

Fill in the table below to help you:

Language feature	Vocabulary	How does this make the Giant's Causeway seem magical?
Use of adjectives		
	Surreal	
		The simile makes us think that the Giant's Causeway is so complex that something magical must have happened to make it form in this way.

40

② Now, using your table as a guide, write at least three paragraphs answering the following question: How does the writer use language in this extract to make the Giant's Causeway seem magical? Here are some sentence starters to help you with your first paragraph:
- Firstly, the writer uses adjectives ...
- For example, ...
- This makes the Giant's Causeway seem magical because ...

③ The writer has used rhetorical questions in the article. What is the effect of these?

FAST FINISHERS
The writer has also used lots of subheadings in the extract. What is the purpose of these subheadings?

NOW TRY THIS

① Imagine that you are Finn McCool. Write a diary entry, from his point of view, describing the fight that he has with Benandonner. Make sure you:
- write in first person narrative
- write about three paragraphs
- describe how the Giant's Causeway was created.

FAST FINISHERS
Write Benandonner's diary. How is it different from Finn McCool's?

② In groups of four, create a TV advert encouraging people to visit the Giant's Causeway. Make sure that you include the following in your advert:
- facts
- information about the legend of Finn McCool
- reasons why people should visit the Giant's Causeway.

PRACTICE QUESTION
Read the extract again. Choose four statements below which are true.
- Copy out the ones that you think are true.
- Choose a maximum of four true statements. [4 Marks]

A The Giant's Causeway is in Scotland. ☐
B The Canyon Wall is green. ☐
C The Causeway is 60 million years old. ☐
D Finn McCool is Scottish. ☐
E There are over 40,000 stone columns. ☐
F Thousands of tourists visit the site every year. ☐
G Benandonner is smaller than Finn McCool. ☐
H The stones form a circular shape. ☐

10 Mulan
From an article on http://disney.fandom.com

▲ Statue of Hua Mulan

LEARNING OBJECTIVES
- To understand new vocabulary.
- To locate and use relevant information from a text.
- To understand the difference between implicit and explicit meaning.

CONTEXT
Mulan is an Ancient Chinese legend. Many years ago, there was a young Chinese girl called Mulan. Her father was sick and frail. However, he had taught his daughter how to ride a horse and use a sword, things that girls didn't traditionally learn about. Government officials came to Mulan's village. They wanted Mulan's father to fight in battle. Mulan knew that if her father fought, he would die, because he was so sick. Mulan secretly disguised herself as a young man and took her father's place. She fought for many years in the Chinese army, even winning a horse and wealth for her bravery. It was only many years later, when she returned home, that people found out that she was a woman, not a man. The article below discusses a new film that has been released about the legend of Mulan. This article is from a website for Disney fans who wish to watch the film, so the writer has used lots of enthusiastic and persuasive language.

Mulan is an upcoming, live-action war action drama film directed by Niki Caro. It is loosely a remake of the 1998 animated feature film, while more based on the original Chinese legend.

> This is the second time that Disney have released a film about Mulan. The first film was not very successful in China. Disney are hoping that this new film will be more successful.

Premise
When The Emperor of China issues a decree that one man per family must serve in the Imperial Army to defend the country from Northern invaders, Hua Mulan, the eldest daughter of an honoured warrior, steps in to take the place of her ailing father. Masquerading as a man, Hua Jun, she is tested every step of the way and must harness her inner-strength and embrace her true potential. It is an epic journey that will transform her into an honoured warrior and earn her the respect of a grateful nation ... and a proud father.

> The adjective 'ailing', shows how unwell and old Mulan's father is.

> The writer uses juxtaposition here. Mulan's father is now 'proud' rather than 'ailing'.

Cast

- Liu Yifei as Hua Mulan
- Donnie Yen as Commander Tung
- Gong Li as Xian Lang, a powerful evil witch
- Jason Scott Lee as Bori Khan, a warrior leader allied with Xian Lang
- Yoson An as Chen Honghui, Mulan's rival who becomes a love interest
- Tzi Ma as Hua Zhou, Mulan's father
- Jet Li as The Emperor of China

> The writer has included a cast list to encourage people to come and watch the film.

Development

The film was announced to be in development on March 30, 2015, to be produced by Chris Bender and J.C. Spike, with a script having been bought from writing team Elizabeth Martin and Lauren Hayneck. On October 4, 2016, the film was confirmed by Disney with a release date set for November 2, 2018. On February 14, 2017, Disney chose Niki Caro to direct the film and Bill Kong as executive producer, due to familiarity of the Chinese culture for the film.

On April 19, 2017, it was reported that Ming-Na Wen, the voice of Mulan in the original film, was in talks to possibly have a cameo in the film. In July 2017, the film's release date was taken off the 2018 calendar with *The Nutcracker and the Four Realms* taking its place. On November 29, 2017, Liu Yifei was cast as Mulan.

On March 1, 2018, the film was pushed back to March 27, 2020. Production on the film began on August 13 along with the release for the first image of Liu Yifei as Mulan. Filming will take place in New Zealand and China. On May 30, it was reported that Mushu [a dragon] will appear.

> Lots of dates have been included here which gives us a great deal of information about the film.

Differences from the 1998 film

- Mulan's family name 'Fa' has been changed to 'Hua', for cultural **authenticity**.
- The character Chen Honghui (played by Yoson An) takes the place of Li Shang in the 1998 film.
- The villain character Bori Khan (played by Jason Scott Lee) takes the place of Shan Yu in the 1998 film.
- Gong Li's evil witch character Xian Lang was created entirely for the film.
- Mulan is an only-child as shown in the 1998 film, while here she is said to have a sister named Hua Xiu (played by Xana Tang). She did have a brother in the original legend.

> The writer has included the main differences between this film and the older version, so that people can look out for these differences when they watch the film.

Trivia

- Actress Gong Li, who will play the evil witch character, Xian Lang, was also the inspiration for the 1998 animated version/counterpart of Mulan.

Non-fiction

▲ The cartoon Mulan

GLOSSARY

Decree: an official order
Ailing: in poor health
Masquerading: pretending
Authenticity: accuracy

SKILLS FOCUS

✔ Understand the content of the article.
✔ Summarise the main information.
✔ Consider the effect of language choices.

LOOK CLOSER

1 This text contains subheadings with lots of information. Fill in the table below which summarises what the different sections are about:

Subheading	Main facts
Premise	
Cast	
Development	
Differences	
Trivia	

2 Now, using your table as a guide, answer the following question:
How does the text suggest that the film will be successful?
Here are some sentence starters to help you:
- One reason I think that this film will be successful is because …
- For example, …
- This suggests that the film will be a success because …

FAST FINISHERS

Does the article make you want to watch the film? Explain your reasons and use evidence from the text to support your point of view.

NOW TRY THIS

1 Do some research on the character Mulan, then write a detailed description of your findings. Make sure that you include:
- information about her family
- famous events that she was involved in
- why she is inspirational.

2 Imagine that you are a journalist writing a news article about the film and have an interview with the actress playing Mulan. What questions would you ask her?

FAST FINISHERS
- Write an account of the day that Mulan disguises herself as a man so that she can fight in the Chinese army.

3 In groups of four, prepare a presentation about a famous, inspirational woman in history. Each person in the group should find out as much as they can about her, her life and why she is an inspiration. Once you have prepared your presentation, present it to the rest of your class.

PRACTICE QUESTION

Write a summary of what this text is about. Your response should:
- cover the main points
- be shorter than the original text.   [8 marks]

◀ Part of the seven-storey pagoda in the Chinese Garden in Singapore, close to the statue of Hua Mulan. In ancient times, pagodas were used as tombs and as a place for offering sacrifices to ancestors.

11 The Loch Ness Monster

From an article in the *Mirror* (online), by John Glover and Tiffany Lo, 25 July 2019

▲ The Loch Ness Monster

LEARNING OBJECTIVES

- To distinguish main ideas and select relevant information from texts.
- To recognise explicit and implicit ideas.
- To show awareness of how language choices affect meaning.

CONTEXT

Legend has it that there is a monster that lives in Loch Ness in Scotland. In the past, some people said they had seen it, but there is no definite proof that the monster actually exists. A photograph was allegedly taken of the monster in 1934, but now it is known that the photograph is a hoax. Below is an article by a man who claims not only to have seen the Loch Ness monster but also to have witnessed another monster swimming next to it.

Loch Ness Monster hunter films 'two 20ft creatures swimming together in water'

Eoin O'Faodhagain says he has spotted the monster four times previously, but it's the first time he has seen two of them next to each other.

A veteran Nessie hunter claimed to have spotted two 20ft monsters swimming together in the famous loch.

Eoin O'Faodhagain, who says he has spotted the mythical creature four times, filmed the moment when two dark objects are seen moving close to the shore.

Eoin, from County Donegal, Northern Ireland, witnessed the rare sightings along with Loch Ness researcher Mikko Takala, who filmed the moment on a webcam, on July 10.

Eoin said: 'The day of the sighting was extremely windy, as you can notice from the trees moving over and back.

The writer suggests that this man is an expert at spotting the monster, but this sighting is even more interesting as there appear to be two monsters.

The adjective 'mythical' suggests that the monster is not real.

The writer discusses the 'rare sightings'. Even though this man has spotted the monster four times previously, most people never see it.

The Loch Ness Monster

'When I noticed the two strange shapes first they were either side of each other and not behind each other, going in the same general direction.

'Never did I think it was two humps from the one animal, the sighting did not give me that impression.'

According to the Nessie spotter, there were two separate objects in the lake and the two shapes were identical to each other.

He guessed the objects were about 20ft long and reaching about 5ft out of the water.

The writer has used statistics here to highlight how big the monsters are.

He added: 'I have never seen two objects so close to each other on the webcam before and I have been watching for years.

'Their shape in the water is very strange. What are they, I don't know. They could be two Nessies.'

About two weeks before the footage, a boat skipper had used sonar to capture an image of a 25ft object deep below the waters in the lake.

Again, the writer has used a statistic here. What is the effect of this?

Mike Bell, from Drumnadrochit, captured the image while he was taking a group of tourists for a trip on Loch Ness on June 27.

The Royal National Lifeboat Institution issued a safety warning on Monday after plans of a mass search for the Loch Ness Monster in September went viral on Facebook.

Lots of people are very interested in searching for the monster.

The RNLI said the water is very deep and has an average temperature of 6C but is prone to deteriorating conditions with wave heights of 4m being recorded.

It would be dangerous to search for the monster.

Research carried out last year revealed that the mythical creature is worth £41m a year to the Scottish economy.

The writer is highlighting how important the monster is for the Scottish economy.

GLOSSARY

Veteran Nessie hunter: someone who has been looking for the monster for a long time

Loch: a lake

County Donegal: a region in North-West Ireland

Skipper: the master of a boat

Sonar: a method of detecting objects underwater using sound pulses

Drumnadrochit: a village on the western shore of Loch Ness

RNLI: the Royal National Lifeboat Institution

Deteriorating: getting worse

Non-fiction

> **SKILLS FOCUS**
> ✔ Identify and interpret information and ideas.
> ✔ Show awareness of how writers use language to achieve effects.

LOOK CLOSER

1. This text contains many short paragraphs with lots of information. Copy and complete the table below to summarise what the paragraphs are about:

Paragraphs	Main facts
1–4	
5–8	
9–12	
13–17	

2. Now read the article again very carefully. In the article, the writers use some important language features:
   - anecdotes (when people discuss their own personal experiences)
   - facts and statistics
   - adjectives.

   Copy and complete the table below, finding an example of each language feature and describing the effect that it has on the reader.

Language feature	Example	Effect on the reader
Anecdote		
Facts/statistics		
Adjectives		

FAST FINISHERS
Can you find any other language features in the extract? What effect do they have on the reader?

The Loch Ness Monster

NOW TRY THIS

1 Imagine that you have just seen the Loch Ness Monster. Write a detailed description of it. What does it look like and what are its features? Copy and complete this table to help you:

	Description
What the monster looks like	
How the monster acts	
How I react to it	

Make sure that you include lots of similes, metaphors and interesting adjectives in your description.

FAST FINISHERS

Do some research on Loch Ness and the Loch Ness Monster. Write a tourist information leaflet encouraging people to visit the area to see the monster.

2 Imagine that you are a reporter who comes to Loch Ness to interview Eoin O'Faodhagain. Prepare questions that you would ask him and the answers that he might give. Once you have done this, find a partner. One of you will be the TV reporter and the other will be Eoin O'Faodhagain. Present your interview to the rest of the class.

PRACTICE QUESTION

How do the writers use language in this extract to interest the reader?
Write at least three paragraphs in response. Here are some sentence starters to help you with your first paragraph:
- One way that the writers use language to interest the reader is ...
- For example, they write ...
- This interests the reader because ...   [8 marks]

12 Robin Hood

From an article on www.historic-uk.com by Ben Johnson

▲ Robin Hood

LEARNING OBJECTIVES

- To distinguish the main ideas in a text.
- To find and list information.
- To analyse the language that the writer uses.

CONTEXT

According to English legend, Robin Hood was an outlaw from Sherwood Forest, in Nottinghamshire, who stole from the rich to give to the poor. His story has become very famous and has led to TV shows and feature films about him. Some historians believe that Robin Hood is based on a real man, Roger Godbeard, who was alive at the same time as 'Robin Hood'. Maid Marion was the woman who Robin Hood was in love with. Below is some information taken from a historical website about Robin Hood.

The writer uses a rhetorical question here so that the reader can think about whether the legend of Robin Hood was actually real.

Legend has it that Robin Hood was an outlaw living in Sherwood Forest with his 'Merry Men' – but did he really exist?

There are several versions of the Robin Hood story. The Hollywood one is that of an incredibly handsome man – Errol Flynn – clothed in garments of Lincoln green, fighting for the rights of the oppressed and outwitting the evil Sheriff of Nottingham.

The writer uses lots of adjectives here to show how glamorous and exciting the Robin Hood legend is.

However the first known literary reference to Robin Hood and his men was in 1377, and the Sloane manuscripts in the British Museum have an account of Robin's life which states that he was born around 1160 in Lockersley (most likely, modern day Loxley) in South Yorkshire. Another chronicler has it that he was a Wakefield man and took part in Thomas of Lancaster's rebellion in 1322.

There are lots of different accounts of Robin Hood's life but we know that someone like him actually did exist.

Robin Hood spent lots of time in both Sherwood Forest and on the coast, in Yorkshire.

One certain fact is that he was a North Country man, with his traditional haunts as an outlaw in Sherwood Forest and a coastal refuge at Robin Hood's Bay in Yorkshire.

The word 'haunts' has more than one meaning. Here, it means a place often visited by Robin Hood.

Robin Hood

One well known story about Robin that places him in Whitby, Yorkshire, is about him and Little John having a friendly archery contest. Both men were skilled at archery and from the roof of the Monastery they both shot an arrow. The arrows fell at Whitby Lathes, more than a mile away. Afterwards the fields where the arrows landed were known as Robin Hood's Close and Little John's Close.

Robin became a popular folk hero because of his generosity to the poor and down-trodden peasants, and his hatred of the Sheriff and his **verderers** who enforced the oppressive forest laws, made him their champion. Some chroniclers date his **exploits** as taking place during the reign of Edward II, but other versions say the king was Richard I, the Lionheart. Robin having fought in the **Crusades** alongside the Lionheart before returning to England to find his lands seized by the Sheriff. *(This account of Robin Hood is different from the myth.)*

All versions of the Robin Hood story give the same account of his death. As he grew older and became ill, he went with Little John to Kirklees Priory near Huddersfield, to be treated by his aunt, the **Prioress**, but a certain Sir Roger de Doncaster persuaded her to murder her nephew and the Prioress slowly bled Robin to death. With the last of his strength he blew his horn and Little John came to his aid, but too late. *(Robin Hood was murdered.)*

Little John placed Robin's bow in his hand and carried him to a window from where Robin managed to **loose one arrow**. Robin asked Little John to bury him where the arrow landed, which he duly did.

A mound in Kirklees Park, within bow-shot of the house, can still be seen and is said to be his last resting place. Little John's grave can be seen in Hathersage churchyard in Derbyshire.

But what of his lover Maid Marion? Not much of Robin's career is known, but nowhere in the chronicles is Maid Marion mentioned, so we must assume she was 'added' to the stories at a later date. *(Maid Marion didn't actually exist.)*

So, Robin did exist, but not in quite the same way as the Robin Hood we all think of, the **cinematic** Robin of Sherwood, Prince of Thieves! His story however, remains one of the best known tales of English folklore.

GLOSSARY

Outlaw: someone who has broken the law

Errol Flynn: a Hollywood actor who played the role of Robin Hood in the 1938 film

Lincoln green: a colour of green dye that comes from Lincoln

Non-fiction

SKILLS FOCUS

- ✓ Find the main ideas in a text.
- ✓ Make inferences based on what has been read.
- ✓ Distinguish between what is true and what is false.

Oppressed: ruled in a cruel way
Outwitting: outsmarting someone
Sloane manuscripts: manuscripts collected by Hans Sloane, a famous doctor, in the 1700s
Chronicler: someone who writes about important historical events
Refuge: a home away from danger
Verderers: officials in England who look after hunting areas that belong to the king or queen
Exploits: bold adventures
Crusades: a series of religious wars in the medieval period
Prioress: a woman in charge of a group of nuns
Loose one arrow: shoot one arrow
Cinematic: the version from the films

LOOK CLOSER

1 Carefully reread Paragraph 2 of the extract.
How has the writer made Robin Hood seem exciting? Think about the use of:
- adjectives
- verbs
- the word 'outwitting'.

Copy and complete the table below to help you:

Language feature	Vocabulary	How does this make Robin Hood seem exciting?
Use of adjectives		
	Fighting for the rights of the oppressed	
		The word 'outwitting' makes the reader think that Robin Hood is a very clever man who is able to use his wits to ensure that good conquers evil.

2 Now, using your table as a guide, write at least three paragraphs answering the following question:
How does the writer, Johnson, use language in this extract to make Robin Hood seem exciting?
Here are some sentence starters to help you with your first paragraph:
- Firstly, the writer uses adjectives …
- For example, …
- This makes Robin Hood seem exciting because …

FAST FINISHERS

Draw a table with two columns, one headed **The myth** and the other **Reality**. Complete with information about how the real Robin Hood is different from the one of legend.

Robin Hood

NOW TRY THIS

1 Write a fact file about Robin Hood, outlining his life and his achievements. Copy and complete the table to help you:

FACT FILE	Robin Hood
Facts about his life, including where he was born	
Main achievements	
Circumstances surrounding his death	

FAST FINISHERS

An obituary is a biography about someone who has died which is usually published in a newspaper shortly after their death. Write a short obituary about Robin Hood. Use your fact file to help you. Remember to:
- write in full sentences
- include facts about his life
- write about why he was so special.

2 In groups of four, create a TV advert encouraging people to visit Nottingham and go on a 'Robin Hood tour'. Make sure that you include the following in your advert:
- facts
- information about the legend of Robin Hood
- reasons why people should visit Nottingham.

❓ PRACTICE QUESTION

Read the extract again. Choose four statements below which are true.
- Copy out the ones that you think are true.
- Choose a maximum of four true statements. **[4 marks]**

A The last known literary reference to Robin Hood and his men was in 1477. ☐
B One certain fact is that he was a North Country man. ☐
C Robin became a popular folk hero because of his generosity to the poor and down-trodden peasants. ☐
D There are many different versions of his death. ☐
E Robin Hood was murdered by his aunt. ☐
F A mound in Kirklees Park is said to be his grave. ☐
G Little John's grave can be seen in Hathersage churchyard in Canterbury. ☐
H Maid Marion is also mentioned in history. ☐

13 The Beast of Bodmin

From an article on **www.cornwalls.co.uk**

▲ Bodmin Moor, Cornwall

LEARNING OBJECTIVES

- To understand the difference between implicit and explicit meaning.
- To locate and use relevant information from a text.
- To understand new vocabulary.

CONTEXT

A famous legend in Cornwall is that of the Beast of Bodmin. Since 1978, there have been many sightings in Bodmin of a 'beast', which people say must be a large wild cat. Some farmers have also said that their animals have been killed by the beast. However, scientists and government officials have done investigations in Bodmin and can find no evidence that the beast actually exists. Below is an article from a tourist website describing the beast.

There is no doubt that Bodmin Moor is a creepy place. Should you happen to find yourself alone there as dusk is falling, try not to think about the layers of legend, horror and mystery associated with this wild and **rugged** landscape, and in particular, whatever you do, try not to let your mind dwell on The Beast.

The Beast is the result of some sixty sightings of a black panther-like big cat, supposedly three to five feet long and sporting white-yellow eyes, combined with numerous reports of mutilated **livestock**. The evidence was robust enough that in 1995 the government ordered an official investigation into the existence of such a beast. The report finally concluded that there was no **verifiable** evidence of a big cat on Bodmin Moor, although it was careful to state that there was no evidence against it, either.

Shortly after the report was published, the public were flabbergasted when a small boy found a leopard skull lying on the banks of the River Fowey. Big cat speculation **reached fever pitch**. Had it escaped from a nearby zoo? Was it the author of the mutilations? The Natural History Museum, boringly, soon found the leopard skull to have been imported into this country as part of a leopardskin rug.

Side annotations:

- The writer uses adjectives and three-part-lists to make Bodmin sound creepy. He also uses capital letters when describing 'The Beast' to make it seem very important.
- The Beast looked like a panther.
- The investigation found that there was no evidence to suggest that The Beast existed.
- The rhetorical questions here show that the existence of The Beast is mysterious.
- The skull did not belong to The Beast at all.

The Beast of Bodmin

Once again, the controversy died down, although sightings were still reported with reasonable regularity, until, in 1998, video footage was released that clearly showed a black animal, probably a big cat, around three and a half feet long. The video, described by a *curator* at Newquay Zoo and wild cat expert as 'the best evidence yet' that big cats do indeed roam Bodmin Moor, was part of another batch of information submitted to the government by local MP, Paul Tyler.

Theories abound. If it does exist (and many swear it does), perhaps the animal is a big cat that escaped a zoo or a private collection and was not reported because it had been imported illegally, a *hypothesis* rejected by scientists on the grounds that the numbers needed to sustain a breeding population would be too large for the food supply. Some believe the animal is a species of wild cat that is believed to have become extinct in Britain more than a hundred years ago. Some, after reading reports not just of hissing and growling but of sounds like a woman screaming, are inclined to blame the *paranormal*. Meanwhile, the sightings continue.

You have been warned!

The writer has used lots of facts here, suggesting that The Beast does actually exist.

The writer gives three suggestions here about what the Beast could actually be.

The author has ended with a one-sentence paragraph and an exclamation mark to highlight how dangerous The Beast is.

GLOSSARY

Rugged: rocky or uneven
Livestock: farm animals
Verifiable: something that can be proved to be true
Reached fever pitch: reached a stage of high excitement
Curator: a keeper of a collection in a museum
Hypothesis: a theory
Paranormal: something beyond normal scientific understanding, such as ghosts

SKILLS FOCUS

✔ Summarise information from a text.
✔ Understand the difference between what is implied and what is stated clearly.

Non-fiction

LOOK CLOSER

1 This text contains six paragraphs with lots of information. Copy and complete the table below to summarise what the paragraphs are about.

Paragraph	Main facts
1	
2	
3	
4	
5	

2 Now, using your table as a guide, write at least three paragraphs answering the following question:
Do you think that the Beast of Bodmin exists? Write your answers using the table below:

Point	Evidence	Explain
One reason I think the Beast exists is that …	For example …	This makes me think that the Beast does exist because …
Another reason I think the Beast exists is that …	For example …	This suggests that …
Finally, I feel that the Beast exists because …	For example …	This makes me think that …

FAST FINISHERS
What evidence is there in the article to suggest that a beast doesn't actually exist?

The Beast of Bodmin

NOW TRY THIS

1 Do some research on the Beast of Bodmin, then write a description of it. Copy and complete the table below to help you.

The Beast's appearance	
How the Beast behaves	
Where the Beast has been sighted	

2 Can you think of any other beasts who are as frightening as the Beast of Bodmin? Write a description of them, using lots of frightening adjectives.

FAST FINISHERS
Pretend you have spotted the Beast. Write a diary entry describing what you saw.

3 In groups of four, prepare a role play/drama where you spot the Beast of Bodmin. What do you all see? What happens as a result of your sighting?

Once you have prepared your role play, perform it to the rest of your class.

? PRACTICE QUESTION

Write a summary of what this text is about. Your response should:
- cover the main points
- be shorter than the original text. [8 marks]

14 Buffy the Vampire Slayer

From an article in the *Guardian* (online), by Vanessa Thorpe, 21 July 2018

▲ Buffy

LEARNING OBJECTIVES

- To distinguish main ideas and select relevant points from a text.
- To recognise explicit and implicit ideas.
- To show awareness of how language choices affect meaning.

CONTEXT

A common European myth is that of vampires. Vampires are corpses that leave their graves at night to find humans. They then suck on the blood of humans with their sharp teeth. *Buffy the Vampire Slayer* was an American TV series about a teenage girl who hunted for vampires and destroyed them. It was very popular in the nineties. The extract below, from an article written in 2018, discusses the possible remake of the show for a modern audience.

Buffy the Vampire Slayer to be remade 21 years after first episode

Unnamed black actor will reportedly take role filled by Sarah Michelle Gellar in 1990s

TV's habit of twinning teenagers with vampires, which became so *voguish* more than twenty years ago with the success of the TV series *Buffy the Vampire Slayer*, just will not lie down and die.

The show, which starred Sarah Michelle Gellar as Buffy and the English actor, Anthony Head, in the role of charming 'watcher' Rupert Giles, is now to be *re-booted*, it has been announced.

According to entertainment industry journal the Hollywood Reporter, an unnamed black actor has been lined up for the lead role in a 'contemporary' version of the story.

The drama, created by Joss Whedon, was first broadcast in 1997 and won *devoted* followers around the world, following as it did in the supernatural wake of the teenage vampire film *The Lost Boys*, a cinematic hit with young audiences a decade earlier in 1987.

- The writer has used personification here to show how TV companies like teenage programmes that have vampires in them.
- The writer has mentioned the original cast and reasons why they have decided to create a new version.
- The adjective 'devoted' suggests that the people who watched the original show were big fans.

Buffy the Vampire Slayer

When Buffy finished battling the undead in 2003, the *Twilight* series of films based on the books of Stephanie Meyer took up the ghostly reins.

> The metaphor 'took up the ghostly reins' links back to the theme of the supernatural in the text.

Whedon will executive produce the series, penned by *Agents of Shield* writer, Monica Owusu-Breen.

However, it seems not everyone is welcoming the reboot.

Writer Michael Patterson tweeted: 'I'm sorry but literally nobody asked for a Buffy reboot. A revival … yes. But not a reboot. The original TV series told a perfect story and did everything it set out to do (revolutionising TV in the process). Why would you mess with such greatness?'

> Some people don't want a new version of the TV programme because they think it will spoil the original.

Author Lilliam Rivera added: 'I loved Buffy. But you know what else I love? When Hollywood looks at new stories by people of colour instead of rebooting old ones and changing the casting.'

Gellar, who played vampire-battling high school student Buffy, recently marked 21 years since the first episode of the show by sharing snaps from behind the scenes.

She told Entertainment Weekly: 'It's the ultimate metaphor: horrors of adolescence manifesting through these actual monsters. It's the hardest time of life.'

> Gellar is saying that being a teenager is tough.

Head recently landed a role as a smooth-talker in Radio 4 soap, *The Archers*.

> Anthony Head is now an actor on the British radio show *The Archers*.

The new series will have a least one new competitor when it arrives. Sky has already released a trailer for the fantasy drama *A Discovery of Witches*, a series based on Deborah Harkness's *All Souls* trilogy of novels.

> *A Discovery of Witches* will be a rival for Buffy.

Scholarly witch Diana Bishop is to be played by Teresa Palmer, while Matthew Goode takes the role of the enigmatic vampire Matthew Clairmont, her romantic interest.

GLOSSARY

Voguish: fashionable
Re-booted: remade
Undead: creatures that are technically dead but are still walking, such as ghosts and vampires
Penned: written
Snaps: photographs
Smooth-talker: someone who can speak very well and often uses this skill to deceive people
Scholarly: intelligent and geeky
Enigmatic: mysterious

Non-fiction

> **SKILLS FOCUS**
> ✔ Locate and use relevant information from a text.
> ✔ Consider the language choices in the text and their effects on the reader.

LOOK CLOSER

1. This text contains a mixture of facts and opinions. Copy and complete the table below, listing some of the facts and opinions used. The first one has been done for you.

Facts	Opinions
Anthony Head starred in the original show	Anthony Head was charming

2. Now read the article again, very carefully. In the article, the writer uses some important language features:
   - facts and statistics
   - adjectives
   - metaphors.

   Copy and complete the table below, finding an example of each language feature and the effect that it has on the reader.

Language feature	Example	Effect on the reader
Facts/statistics		
Adjectives		
Metaphors		

FAST FINISHERS
Can you find any other language features in the extract? What effect do they have on the reader?

Buffy the Vampire Slayer

NOW TRY THIS

1 Imagine that you have just seen a vampire. Write a detailed description of it. What does it look like and what are its features? Fill in a table like the one below to help you.

Appearance of vampire	
Actions of vampire	
My reaction to vampire	

Make sure that you include lots of similes, metaphors and interesting adjectives in your description.

FAST FINISHERS

Do some research on the history of vampires. Write a fact file about them which you can share with others.

2 In groups of four, imagine that you are going on a vampire hunt. Prepare a TV documentary telling people about the vampire hunt. Consider:
- how you have to prepare for vampire hunting
- the vampire hunt itself
- the outcome of the vampire hunt.

Show your documentary to the rest of the class.

❓ PRACTICE QUESTION

How does the writer use language in this extract to interest the reader?

Write at least three paragraphs in response. Here are some sentence starters to help you with your first paragraph:
- One way that the writer uses language to interest the reader is …
- For example, she writes …
- This interests the reader because …   [8 marks]

15 Greek Giants
From an article on www.amnh.org

▲ The giant Antaeus

LEARNING OBJECTIVES
- To distinguish the main ideas.
- To retrieve explicit and implicit information.
- To analyse the writer's use of language.

CONTEXT
There are many myths and legends about giants. Below is an extract from an informative article on the website of The American Museum of Natural History, which outlines some of the different giants and why people might think that giants exist.

'Before there were any humans on **Pallene**, the story goes that a battle was fought between the gods and the giants. Traces of the giants' **demise** continue to be seen to this day, whenever torrents swell with rain and excessive water breaks their banks and floods the fields. They say that even now in gullies and ravines the people discover bones of immeasurable enormity, like men's **carcasses** but far bigger.'

Greek historian Solinus, c. AD 200

The Ancient Greeks believed that giants existed. This is an extract of an account written by a Greek historian in AD 200.

Gigantic bones

The ancient Greeks told stories of giants, describing them as flesh-and-blood creatures who lived and died – and whose bones could be found coming out of the ground where they were buried long ago. Indeed, even today, large and surprisingly human-like bones can be found in Greece. Modern scientists understand such bones to be the remains of mammoths, **mastodons**, and woolly rhinoceroses that once lived in the region.

The writer uses listing here to show the kind of bones that were often mistaken for the bones of giants.

But ancient Greeks were largely unfamiliar with these massive animals, and many believed that the enormous bones they found were the remains of human-like giants. Any nonhuman traits in the bones were thought to be due to the **grotesque** anatomical features of giants.

Ancient Greeks were unfamiliar with large animals, often mistaking them for giants.

Greek Giants

At a glance: giant

From Paul Bunyan of American folklore to the Norse creator-god Ymir, human-like giants populate the myths of many cultures.

- The long bones of elephant relatives and humans are similar enough to be confused.
- Geological events tend to destroy the skulls of prehistoric elephant relatives, leaving only enormous, human-like long bones, ribs, and vertebrae.
- Ancient authors often reported finding the remains of giants hundreds of feet tall – much bigger than an elephant or any other animal. These reports may represent attempts to reconstruct the bones of several animals found jumbled together as a single giant.

…

Seeing is believing

The people of Tingis (modern-day Tangier, Morocco) once boasted that their city's founder was a giant named Antaeus who was buried in a mound south of town. To test the claim, Roman soldiers dug into the mound in 81BC. Much to their surprise, an enormous skeleton surfaced – which they then reburied with great honours. Modern scientists confirm that ancient elephant fossils are common in the area.

A giant's bridge?

The spectacular Giant's Causeway on the northeast coast of Ireland consists of about 40,000 interlocking columns of basalt rock. According to Irish myth, the Irish giant Finn MacCool built the causeway so he could walk to Scotland to fight the Scottish giant Benandonner. Formations like this one are typically the result of volcanic activity. Some 65 million years ago, lava flowed over the area. As the lava cooled, it contracted, fracturing into the columns seen today.

The writer has used bullet points and listing here to break up each section of the text.

Scientists believed that the Giant's Causeway was formed from cooling lava.

The Romans dug up a skeleton which they thought was a giant.

GLOSSARY

Pallene: a region of Northern Greece
Demise: downfall and death
Carcasses: skeletons
Mastodons: an extinct, elephant-like mammal
Grotesque: ugly and distorted
Paul Bunyan: a giant lumberjack in American myth
Norse creator-god Ymir: a giant in Norse mythology

Non-fiction

> **SKILLS FOCUS**
>
> ✔ Find the main ideas in the text.
> ✔ Make inferences based on what has been read.
> ✔ Distinguish between what is true and what is false.

LOOK CLOSER

1 Re-read the first paragraph. How has the writer made this section of the text exciting? Think about the use of:
- adjectives
- verbs
- the word 'carcasses'.

Fill in a copy of the table below to help you.

Language feature	Vocabulary	How does this make the text exciting?
Use of adjectives		
	Fought Breaks Swell Floods	
		The word 'carcasses' makes this extract seem frightening and quite gruesome. It seems a lot more exciting than using the word 'bones'.

2 Now, using your table as a guide, answer the following question:
How does the writer use language in this extract to make it exciting?
Here are some sentence starters to help you:
- Firstly, the writer uses adjectives …
- For example, …
- This makes the extract seem exciting because …

FAST FINISHERS
There are many giants in fiction and poetry, and many articles about giants. Write a list of all the giants that you can think of and give some information about their origins.

Greek Giants

NOW TRY THIS

1 Write a factual leaflet for primary school children about giants and their origins. Make sure that you include the following in your leaflet:

- subheadings
- facts about giants and what they could actually be
- pictures.

Make sure that you use clear expressions so that young children can understand your points.

FAST FINISHERS

Do some research about a giant of your choice and write a fact file about it.

2 There are many giants, such as Finn McCool, the Cyclops, and the Jolly Green Giant. Who is your favourite giant? Prepare a presentation for the rest of the class outlining who your favourite giant is and why. Make sure that you include the following in your advert:

- facts about your favourite giant
- reasons why they are your favourite giant.

You might wish to read Extracts 2 and 9 to help you with this!

PRACTICE QUESTION

Read the extract again. Choose four statements below which are true.

- Copy out the ones that you think are true.
- Choose a maximum of four true statements. [4 marks]

A Even today large and surprisingly human-like bones can be found in Greece. ☐
B These bones are actually dinosaur bones. ☐
C The bones could belong to several animals. ☐
D Tangier is in France. ☐
E When Roman soldiers dug up Tingis, they found an enormous skeleton. ☐
F The Giant's Causeway consists of about 60,000 interlocking columns of basalt rock. ☐
G Giants did actually exist. ☐
H Most stories about giants can be explained by scientific facts. ☐

16 Aphrodite
From a travel website

▲ Paphos in Cyprus

LEARNING OBJECTIVES
- To show awareness of persuasive techniques.
- To analyse persuasive language used in the text.
- To use appropriate references.

CONTEXT
In Ancient Greek myth, Aphrodite was the Greek goddess of love. She is mentioned by the Greek poet Hesiod in 650BC. It is said that she came from the island of Paphos in Cyprus. Below is an extract from a travel website which is encouraging people to visit the island.

Paphos, a historical resort on the coast of the island of Cyprus, has an abundance on offer for tourists. You'll find ancient historical sites, beautiful hidden coves, scenic beaches and a huge choice of places to dine and drink. You can visit at any time of the year as the resort boasts hot and sunny weather almost all year round and even in the winter it is warm and pleasant.

Culture and history
You can't beat Paphos for a cultural experience. Thousands of holidaymakers are drawn year after year to the resort, which is full of ancient wonders. Just a few of the places visitors should see include the Tombs of the Kings, the famous castle on the harbour and the breath-taking birthplace of the Greek goddess Aphrodite. That's not to mention the enormous archaeological park brimming with prehistoric treasures.

Going out
You won't be stuck for bars and restaurants in Paphos. The harbour is the place to be to find an excellent choice of places to dine and drink. Have a bite to eat or enjoy a refreshing KEO from one of the many waterfront bars and cafes after you enjoy a walk along

---

The writer has used many positive adjectives here to persuade people to visit Paphos: 'hot', 'sunny', 'warm', 'pleasant' and 'beautiful'.

The writer uses alliteration in the phrase 'breath-taking birthplace' here.

The verb 'brimming' shows that there are plenty of prehistoric remains in the archaeological park.

The writer lists all of the activities that you can do in Paphos at night time.

the promenade. If a big night out is what you are after, try Agiou Antoniou Street, where you'll find the highest density of bars in the city. It is so famous for its nightlife that it is also known as 'Bar Street' or 'Nightlife Street'.

Activities

Paphos is not just about history and nightlife. It's a brilliant destination for families as there's a whole host of activities on offer to keep everyone occupied. Find your way to Coral Bay to relax on its excellent beach and make the most of the water sports on offer or seek out high-speed thrills at the Paphos Karting Centre. For non-stop fun, have the ultimate family day out at the Paphos Aphrodite Waterpark.

> Adjectives such as 'excellent' and 'ultimate' are used to show what an amazing place Paphos is.

The weather

Mediterranean weather is very hot in the summer and mild in the winter, and Paphos is no exception. Summer officially starts in June with temperatures of 23°C which rise to a peak of 26°C in August. Humidity is low and comfortable. The skies are clear and blue for most of the summer with up to 14 hours of bright sunshine every day. On the coast, where the seawater is 27°C, you'll be cooled off by the breeze flowing in from the Mediterranean Sea.

If you prefer cooler temperatures, you might like to visit Paphos in the autumn. Many visitors want to avoid the scorching heat of the summer but still take advantage of the warm and sunny weather. In the autumn, the daily average is a pleasant 22°C with lows of 16°C.

> The writer has used lots of statistics to highlight how pleasant the weather is.

The winter is mild in Paphos. By November, temperatures range from 8°C to 19°C. January is the coldest month of the year but the average temperature is still very comfortable at 13°C. Rainfall also starts to pick up in the winter. November has 66mm over the month which rises to 94mm by December.

By the spring, the weather improves once more and there is very little rain. The Troodos Mountains help to keep weather conditions dry and pleasant all year round by providing extra shelter from cold winds.

> Adjectives such as 'dry' and 'pleasant' are used to describe the weather.

Non-fiction

GLOSSARY

Tombs of the Kings: ancient underground burial sites near Cyprus
KEO: a type of beer
Promenade: the pavement by a seafront

SKILLS FOCUS

✔ Analyse the language used in the extract.
✔ Consider the ways this extract tries to persuade the reader.
✔ Use a range of persuasive techniques.

LOOK CLOSER

1. Read Paragraph 1 of the text. How does the writer encourage you to want to visit Paphos? Copy and complete the table below to help you. The first row has been done for you.

Vocabulary	Language feature	How does this encourage you to want to visit Paphos?
boasts	Verb and personification	This suggests that Paphos has got a lot to show off about.
hot and sunny weather		
warm and pleasant		
beautiful hidden coves		
ancient historical sites		
huge choice of places to dine and drink		

2. Now, using your table as a guide, write at least three paragraphs answering the following question:
   How does the writer use language in this extract to make you want to visit Paphos?
   Here are some sentence starters to help you with your first paragraph:
   - Firstly, the writer uses interesting verbs …
   - For example, …
   - This makes the reader want to visit Paphos because …

FAST FINISHERS

Have a look at Paragraph 2. How has the writer used language here to make it seem exciting?
Fill in a table like the one below to help you.

Aphrodite

Vocabulary	Language feature	How does this make it seem exciting?

NOW TRY THIS

1 Turn the information you have gathered above into a tourist information leaflet about Paphos. Make sure that you include the following in your leaflet:
- subheadings
- facts about Aphrodite and her link to Paphos
- pictures.

Make sure that you write the leaflet persuasively so that readers will be encouraged to visit the island of Paphos.

FAST FINISHERS
Undertake some research about a Greek island of your choice and write a fact file about it.

2 In groups of four, prepare a TV advert encouraging people to visit Paphos. Make sure that you include the following in your advert:
- facts
- information about Paphos
- reasons why people should visit Paphos.

Be ready to show your advert to the rest of the class.

? PRACTICE QUESTION

Read Paragraphs 3 and 4 of the extract, 'Going out' and 'Activities'. How has the writer used language to encourage the reader to want to visit Paphos?

Write at least three paragraphs in response. Here are some sentence starters to help you with your first paragraph:
- Firstly, the writer uses …
- For example, they write …
- This encourages the reader to want to visit Paphos because … [8 marks]

69

Section 3: Poetry

17 The Kraken
By Alfred Lord Tennyson, 1830

▲ Drawing of a colossal octopus by Pierre Denys de Montfort

LEARNING OBJECTIVES
- To distinguish the main ideas and select relevant points from the texts.
- To recognise explicit and implicit ideas.
- To show awareness of how language choices affect meaning.

CONTEXT
In legend, the Kraken was a sea monster that was said to swallow ships off the coast of Norway. The monster was said to be so powerful that it created a whirlpool that would suck even the largest ships to the seabed. The Kraken was first mentioned in a book called *A History of Norway* in 1752, when a gigantic squid was spotted. Alfred Lord Tennyson, a very famous Victorian poet, wrote a poem about the monster in 1830.

Below the thunders of the **upper deep**;
Far, far beneath in the **abysmal** sea,
His ancient, dreamless, uninvaded sleep
The Kraken **sleepeth**: faintest **sunlights** flee
About his **shadowy sides**: above him swell
Huge **sponges** of **millennial growth** and height;
And far away into the **sickly** light,
From many a wondrous **grot** and **secret cell**
Unnumbered and enormous **polypi**
Winnow with giant arms the slumbering green.
There hath he lain for ages and will lie
Battening upon huge sea-worms in his sleep,
Until the **latter fire** shall heat the deep;
Then once by man and angels to be seen,
In **roaring** he shall rise and on the surface die.

Annotations (left):
- The light is distant as it is coming from the surface of the sea.
- Tennyson is describing the movement of the polypi at the bottom of the sea.
- The Kraken is still sleeping.
- The monster will wake when the world ends.

Annotations (right):
- The Kraken's home is very deep in the sea. Tennyson uses adjectives such as 'abysmal' to emphasise how deeply below the sea his home is.
- Tennyson uses a three-part list here to show the reader that the Kraken has been sleeping for a very long time.
- Tennyson uses sibilance, the repetition of the 'S' sound, over a few lines here. What is the effect of this?
- Tennyson uses the verb 'roaring' to show how loud the Kraken will be when he wakes up, comes to the surface, and then dies.

The Kraken

GLOSSARY

Upper deep: the surface of the sea
Abysmal: very deep
Millennial growth: the creature has been growing for a thousand years
Sickly: weak
Grot: grotto / small cave
Secret cell: secret cave
Polypi: unmoving sea animal with a body like a tube
Winnow: fan
Battening: feeding himself
Latter fire: the end of the world

SKILLS FOCUS

✔ Understand the ideas in the poem.
✔ Analyse the language used in the poem.
✔ Analyse the structure of the poem.

LOOK CLOSER

1. Read the poem again. Now draw a storyboard summarising what happens in the poem. Use a copy of the table below to help you.

1)	2)
The Kraken sleepeth	Enormous polypi winnow
3)	4)
Battening upon huge sea-worms in his sleep	In roaring he shall rise

Poetry

2 The poem contains some important language features. Copy and fill in the table below, analysing the language that Tennyson uses. The first row has been done for you.

Vocabulary	Language feature	How does this make the reader feel?
Below the thunders of the upper deep; Far, far beneath in the abysmal sea,	Adjectives	The reader will feel intrigued about what lies deep below the surface of the sea.
His ancient, dreamless, uninvaded sleep	Three-part list	
faintest sunlights flee About his shadowy sides	Sibilance	
From many a wondrous grot and secret cell Unnumbered and enormous polypi Winnow with giant arms the slumbering green		
Battening upon huge sea-worms in his sleep		
In roaring he shall rise and on the surface die.		

FAST FINISHERS
- Have a look at the structure of the poem.
    - What happens at the beginning of the poem?
    - How does this change in the middle of the poem?
    - How does the poem end?
- Why do you think that Tennyson has chosen to structure the poem in this way?

Make sure that you use full sentences when you answer these questions.

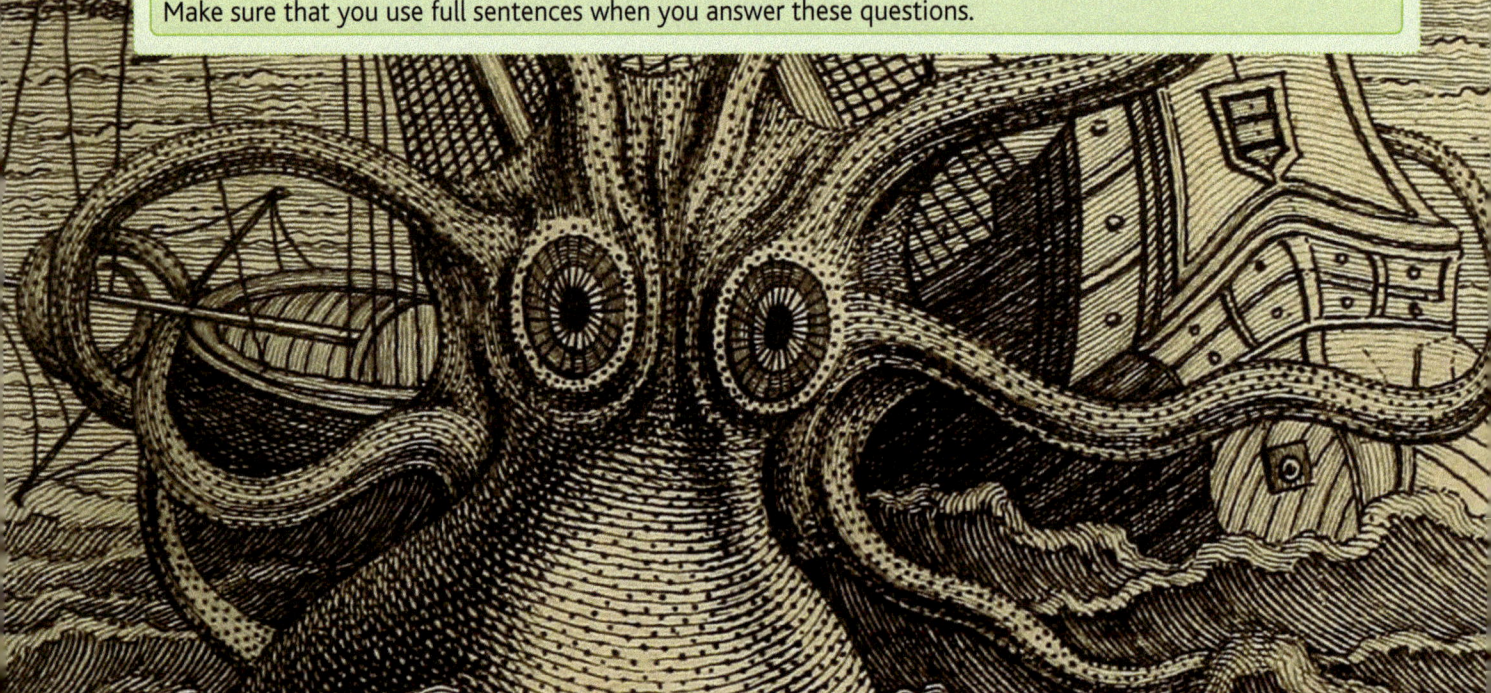

The Kraken

NOW TRY THIS

1 Using the information in the poem, write your own fact file about the Kraken. You could start the fact file like this:

Name of monster	Kraken
Height	
Weight	
Age	
Colour	
Interesting features	
Special qualities	

Make sure that you also draw a picture of the Kraken to go in your fact file.

FAST FINISHERS

Create your own sea monster and write a fact file about it.

2 Imagine that you are sailing on a ship in the sea and come face-to-face with the Kraken. In groups of four, prepare a role play to perform to the rest of the class. One of you can be the Kraken and the rest of you can be sailors on the ship. Make sure that your role play is exciting and dramatic. You may wish to use music and props to make the drama more exciting.

PRACTICE QUESTION

Read the poem again. How has Tennyson used language to make the Kraken seem frightening? Write at least three paragraphs in response. Here are some sentence starters to help you with your first paragraph:

- Firstly Tennyson uses …
- For example, he writes …
- This makes the Kraken seem frightening because … [8 marks]

18 Robin Hood

By John Keats, 1820

LEARNING OBJECTIVES
- To find and list information.
- To analyse the language of the poem.
- To consider the cultural context of the poem.

CONTEXT

John Keats was a poet who was born in 1795 and died in 1821, when he was just 25 years old. He wrote many poems about nature, but also enjoyed writing about myths and legends, such as the poem below about Robin Hood. Throughout the poem, the speaker is sad that Robin Hood no longer exists. Keats may also be sad about the modern world, wishing that he could go back in time to a place where life was happier and simpler, and people weren't obsessed with money.

No! those days are gone away
And their hours are old and gray,
And their minutes buried all
Under the down-trodden **pall** ◁──── The speaker is suggesting that the happy time of Robin Hood has now gone.
Of the leaves of many years:

Keats mentions winter which gives the poem a depressing tone. ────▷ Many times have **winter's shears**, ◁────
Frozen North, and chilling East,
Sounded **tempests** to the feast
Of the forest's **whispering fleeces**, ◁──── Keats uses sibilance (the repetition of the S sound) to highlight the sound of the forest's whispering fleeces.

The speaker is discussing rent and finances. He is saying that in the time of Robin Hood, these things were not as important as they are now, and life was much simpler. ────▷ Since men knew nor rent nor leases.

  No, the **bugle** sounds no more,
And the twanging bow no more;
Silent is the ivory shrill ◁──── Again, Keats has used sibilance here.
Past the heath and up the hill;
There is no mid-forest laugh,

Echo is explored in Extract 8. ────▷ Where lone **Echo** gives the half
To some **wight**, amaz'd to hear
Jesting, deep in **forest drear**. ◁──── Keats writes about how the forest is now sad and empty.

  On the fairest time of June
You may go, with sun or moon,
Or the seven stars to light you,
Or the polar ray to right you;

Robin Hood

But you never may behold
Little John, or Robin bold;
Never one, of all the clan,
Thrumming on an empty can
Some old hunting ditty, while
He doth his green way beguile
To fair hostess Merriment,
Down beside the pasture Trent;
For he left the merry tale
Messenger for spicy ale.

  Gone, the merry morris din;
Gone, the song of Gamelyn;
Gone, the tough-belted outlaw
Idling in the 'grenè shawe';
All are gone away and past!
And if Robin should be cast
Sudden from his turfed grave,
And if Marian should have
Once again her forest days,
She would weep, and he would craze:
He would swear, for all his oaks,
Fall'n beneath the dockyard strokes,
Have rotted on the briny seas;
She would weep that her wild bees
Sang not to her—strange! that honey
Can't be got without hard money!

  So it is: yet let us sing,
Honour to the old bow-string!
Honour to the bugle-horn!
Honour to the woods unshorn!
Honour to the Lincoln green!
Honour to the archer keen!
Honour to tight little John,
And the horse he rode upon!
Honour to bold Robin Hood,
Sleeping in the underwood!
Honour to maid Marian,
And to all the Sherwood-clan!
Though their days have hurried by
Let us two a burden try.

- Keats is saying that even on a sunny day you'll no longer see Robin Hood.
- Keats continues to mourn the loss of Robin Hood.
- Keats is repeating the word 'gone' to emphasise that Robin Hood no longer exists.
- Keats is writing about how you have to pay for everything now, whereas during the time of Robin Hood life was happy and things such as honey were free.
- Keats is repeating the word 'honour' to show how much he respects the characters of the old legend.

Poetry

▲ John Keats (1795–1821)

GLOSSARY

Pall: a cloth spread over a coffin
Tempests: storms
Whispering fleeces: leaves of the forest
Bugle: a small trumpet without keys
Wight: person
Ditty: song
Beguile: charm
Morris: an English dance
Gamelyn: the son of the old man
Grenè shawe: green wood
Turfed grave: grave covered in grass
Briny: salty
Unshorn: uncut
Lincoln green: a shade of green worn by Robin Hood
Underwood: small trees growing underneath taller ones

SKILLS FOCUS

✔ Summarise the poem.
✔ List information.
✔ Consider the reasons why Keats might have written the poem.

LOOK CLOSER

1. Read the poem again. Draw a concept map containing all of the things that Keats is complaining about in the poem. Find a quotation for each one. For example, he complains about how everything costs money.

Everything comes at a price.
*strange! that honey
Can't be got without hard money!*

Robin Hood

2 Now write the poem again in the form of a letter in modern English. Remember that you are complaining about how terrible life is now, compared to the time of Robin Hood. Here are some sentence starters to help you:
- Life used to be so good …
- The forest with Robin Hood in it was such fun …
- Everybody used to dance …
- Now everyone has to pay rent …
- Everything costs money now …

FAST FINISHERS
- Have a look at the structure of the poem.
  - How does the poem begin?
  - What happens in the middle?
  - How does the tone change at the end?
- Why do you think that Keats has chosen to structure the poem in this way?

Make sure that you use full sentences when you answer these questions.

NOW TRY THIS

1 Choose a historical person or someone from legend that you admire. Now write your own poem about them. Try to use some of the following techniques in your poem:
- repetition
- simile or metaphor
- descriptive adjectives.

Your poem doesn't have to rhyme!

FAST FINISHERS
Do some research on John Keats. Who was he? What was life like at the time that he wrote the poem? Why do you think that he wrote it? Write three paragraphs summarising your research.

2 Think of something in the modern day that really bothers you. Write a speech outlining what it is. Make sure that you include the following in your speech:
- an engaging opening
- reasons why you are so bothered about this
- a memorable ending.

Once you have written and rehearsed your speech, share it with the rest of the class.

❓ PRACTICE QUESTION

Read the final verse of the poem again. List four things that the speaker 'honours' in this verse. [4 marks]

19 The Lady of Shalott

By Alfred Lord Tennyson, 1832

'The Lady of Shalott' by William Holman Hunt

LEARNING OBJECTIVES

- To distinguish the main ideas and select relevant points from the texts.
- To recognise explicit and implicit ideas.
- To explore the writer's presentation of character.

CONTEXT

'The Lady of Shalott' is about a woman who lives on an island called Shalott, near Camelot, the home of King Arthur. She lives in a tower and is cursed. She is not able to look out of the window at the town of Camelot, because if she does that, she will die. Instead, the Lady of Shalott looks at the town through a mirror. One day, Sir Lancelot the knight rides by on a horse. The Lady of Shalott is fascinated with him so turns around and looks at him through the window. The mirror cracks and the curse comes upon her. The Lady of Shalott takes a small boat and floats through Camelot, where she dies. 'The Lady of Shalott' is one of Tennyson's most famous poems and there are many paintings depicting her. This is the first part of the poem.

Part I

On either side the river lie
Long fields of barley and of rye,
That clothe the wold and meet the sky;
And thro' the field the road runs by
   To many-tower'd Camelot;
The yellow-leaved waterlily
The green-sheathed daffodilly
Tremble in the water chilly
   Round about Shalott.

Willows whiten, aspens shiver.
The sunbeam showers break and quiver
In the stream that runneth ever

Tennyson uses adjectives to describe the brightness of the flowers.

Camelot is in the countryside. Tennyson is giving us a detailed description of the setting.

The personification here makes the flowers seem alive.

The Lady of Shalott

By the island in the river
  Flowing down to Camelot.
Four gray walls, and four gray towers
Overlook a space of flowers,
And the silent isle **imbowers**
  The Lady of Shalott.

Underneath the bearded barley,
The **reaper**, reaping late and early,
Hears her ever chanting cheerly,
Like an angel, singing clearly,
  O'er the stream of Camelot.
Piling the sheaves in furrows airy,
Beneath the moon, the reaper weary
Listening whispers, 'Tis the fairy,
  Lady of Shalott.'

The little isle is all **inrail'd**
With a rose-fence, and overtrail'd
With roses: by the **marge unhail'd**
The shallop flitteth silken sail'd,
  Skimming down to Camelot.
A pearl garland winds her head:
She leaneth on a velvet bed,
Full royally apparelled,
  The Lady of Shalott.

Tennyson has used the word 'imbowers' to show that the Lady of Shalott is trapped.

Tennyson is saying that the Lady of Shalott sings like an angel.

Despite her situation, the Lady of Shalott seems happy.

The reaper calls the Lady of Shalott a 'fairy'.

The Lady of Shalott is dressed like royalty.

GLOSSARY

Wold: countryside
Aspens: a type of tree
Imbowers: encloses
Reaper: a person who harvests the crops
Inrail'd: enclosed
Marge unhail'd / The shallop flitteth silken sail'd: the small boat outside her castle is moving in the wind

▲ 'The Lady of Shalott' by John William Waterhouse

Poetry

> **SKILLS FOCUS**
>
> ✔ Understand and summarise the poem.
> ✔ Explore the character of the Lady of Shalott.
> ✔ Analyse Tennyson's use of language.

LOOK CLOSER

1. Read the poem again. Based on your reading of the poem, draw a map showing where The Lady of Shalott is and where the other parts of Camelot are. Make sure that you include the following:
   - the castle
   - the boat
   - the reapers
   - the trees
   - the river
   - the stream
   - the plants
   - the flowers.

2. The poem contains some important language features. Copy and fill in the table below, analysing the language that Tennyson uses.

Vocabulary	Language feature	How does this make the reader feel?
The yellow-leaved waterlily The green-sheathed daffodilly Tremble in the water chilly	Adjectives	
Willows whiten, aspens shiver. The sunbeam showers break and quiver	Personification	
Hears her ever chanting cheerly, Like an angel, singing clearly,	Simile	

3. Have a look at the structure of the first part of the poem.
   - How does Tennyson set the scene?
   - What is he describing in the middle?
   - How does the mood change at the end of the poem?

The Lady of Shalott

4 Why do you think that Tennyson has chosen to structure the poem in this way?
Make sure that you use full sentences when you answer these questions.

FAST FINISHERS

This is only one part of the poem. Use the internet to find and read the rest of the poem. What happens to The Lady of Shalott?

NOW TRY THIS

1 Using the information in this part of the poem, write a diary entry for the Lady of Shalott. How does she feel being stuck in the tower? You may start your diary like this:

> Dear Diary,
>
> It has been 18 years since I became imprisoned in this tower. I haven't been outside in all that time …

Make sure that you write in first person narrative and use paragraphs when writing your diary.

FAST FINISHERS

How did the Lady of Shalott die? Do some research and then write a newspaper report about her death. Make sure that you include the following in your report:
- a catchy headline
- eyewitness accounts
- a picture.

Remember the 5 Ws. What happened? Where did it happen? Who did it happen to? When did it happen? Why did it happen?

2 There have been many paintings of the Lady of Shalott. In groups of four, search for some of the paintings online, then choose one painting that depicts her and prepare a presentation about the painting. Think about the following:
- Who is the artist?
- What is interesting about the painting?
- Which part of the poem is the painting about?
- How does the Lady of Shalott come across in this painting?

Share your presentation with the rest of the class.

PRACTICE QUESTION

Read the poem again. How has Tennyson used language to make the poem interesting? Write at least three paragraphs in response. Here are some sentence starters to help you with your first paragraph:
- Firstly Tennyson uses …
- For example, he writes …
- This makes the poem interesting because … [8 marks]

20 Near Avalon

By William Morris, 1858

> **LEARNING OBJECTIVES**
> - To distinguish the main ideas and select relevant points from the texts.
> - To recognise explicit and implicit ideas.
> - To show awareness of how language choices affect meaning.

> **CONTEXT**
> A famous female in legends about King Arthur is Guinevere. There are lots of different stories about her. She was married to King Arthur and many stories suggest that she was kidnapped or had an affair with Sir Lancelot. King Arthur went to battle and eventually brought Guinevere back home, but his kingdom fell as a result. The poem below, by William Morris, explores this. William Morris was a textile designer and poet who lived in the Victorian era. In legend, Avalon is said to be the final home of King Arthur, situated where Glastonbury is today.

▲ 'Lancelot and Guinevere' painted by Herbert James Draper

Near Avalon

> A ship with shields before the sun,
> Six maidens round the mast,
> A red-gold crown on every one,
> A green gown on the last.
>
> The fluttering green banners there
> Are wrought with ladies' heads most fair,
> And a portraiture of Guinevere
> The middle of each sail doth bear.
>
> A ship with sails before the wind,
> And round the helm six knights,
> Their heaumes are on, whereby, half blind,
> They pass by many sights.
>
> The tatter'd scarlet banners there
> Right soon will leave the spear-heads bare.
> Those six knights sorrowfully bear
> In all their heaumes some yellow hair.

Annotations:
- Guinevere is wearing a green gown to show she is different from the other maidens. → *A green gown on the last.*
- Morris uses the adjectives 'fluttering' and 'green' when describing the banners. → *The fluttering green banners there*
- There is a portrait of Guinevere on each of the sails because the knights have rescued her. → *And a portraiture of Guinevere / The middle of each sail doth bear.*
- Morris describes the knights as 'half-blind' because they can't see as their helmets are so low on their heads. → *half blind*
- The knights have been in battle so the banners are 'tatter'd'. → *The tatter'd scarlet banners there*
- The spear-heads are no longer in use because the knights are no longer fighting. → *Right soon will leave the spear-heads bare.*
- The knights carry Guinevere's yellow hair. → *In all their heaumes some yellow hair.*

GLOSSARY

Heaumes: a medieval helmet
Spear-heads: the head of a spear; in medieval times spears were often used in battle

SKILLS FOCUS

- ✔ Understand the ideas in the poem.
- ✔ Analyse Morris' use of language.
- ✔ Analyse the structure of the poem.

Poetry

LOOK CLOSER

1) Read the poem again. Now draw a storyboard summarising what happens in the poem. Use the table below to help you. Use one box for each stanza.

1)	2)
A ship with shields before the sun, / Six maidens round the mast,	
3)	4)

2) The poem contains some very effective language features. Copy and fill in the table below analysing the language that Morris uses. The first row has been done for you.

Vocabulary	Language feature	How does this make the reader feel?
A ship with shields before the sun, Six maidens round the mast	Sibilance	The repetition of the 'S' sounds could reflect the sound of the sea. This could make the reader feel calm and peaceful, as if they are sailing on the ocean themselves.
The fluttering green banners	Adjectives	
Half blind	Metaphor	
Tatter'd scarlet banners		

FAST FINISHERS

Have a look at the structure of the poem and answer the following questions:
- What is the atmosphere like at the start of the poem?
- How is the atmosphere different at the end?
- Why do you think that the mood has changed so much?

Make sure that you use full sentences when you answer these questions.

Near Avalon

NOW TRY THIS

1. Using the information in the poem, write your own description of the ship. Include the following information:
   - the appearance of the ship
   - where the ship has gone and where it is going
   - who is on the ship.

   Make sure that you write using full sentences, descriptive adjectives and language features such as similes and metaphors.

   FAST FINISHERS
   Where do you think that the ship went? Write a paragraph explaining your views. You may begin like this:
   I think that the ship is going to _____ because …

2. There are many stories set during the time of King Arthur. In groups of four, do some research on the legend of King Arthur. Choose one story and share it with the rest of the class. Try to make your retelling of the story exciting and dramatic, and make sure that each person in your group participates.

❓ PRACTICE QUESTION

Read the poem again. How has Morris structured the poem to interest the reader? Write three paragraphs. Here are some sentence starters to help you:

- **Paragraph 1**
  At the start of the poem there is a _____ mood.
  For example, Morris writes …
  This makes the poem interesting because …
- **Paragraph 2**
  In the middle of the poem the mood changes and becomes …
  For example, Morris writes …
  This is interesting because …
- **Paragraph 3**
  Finally, at the end of the poem the mood is _____.
  For example, Morris writes …
  I think the mood has changed from the beginning because …   [8 marks]

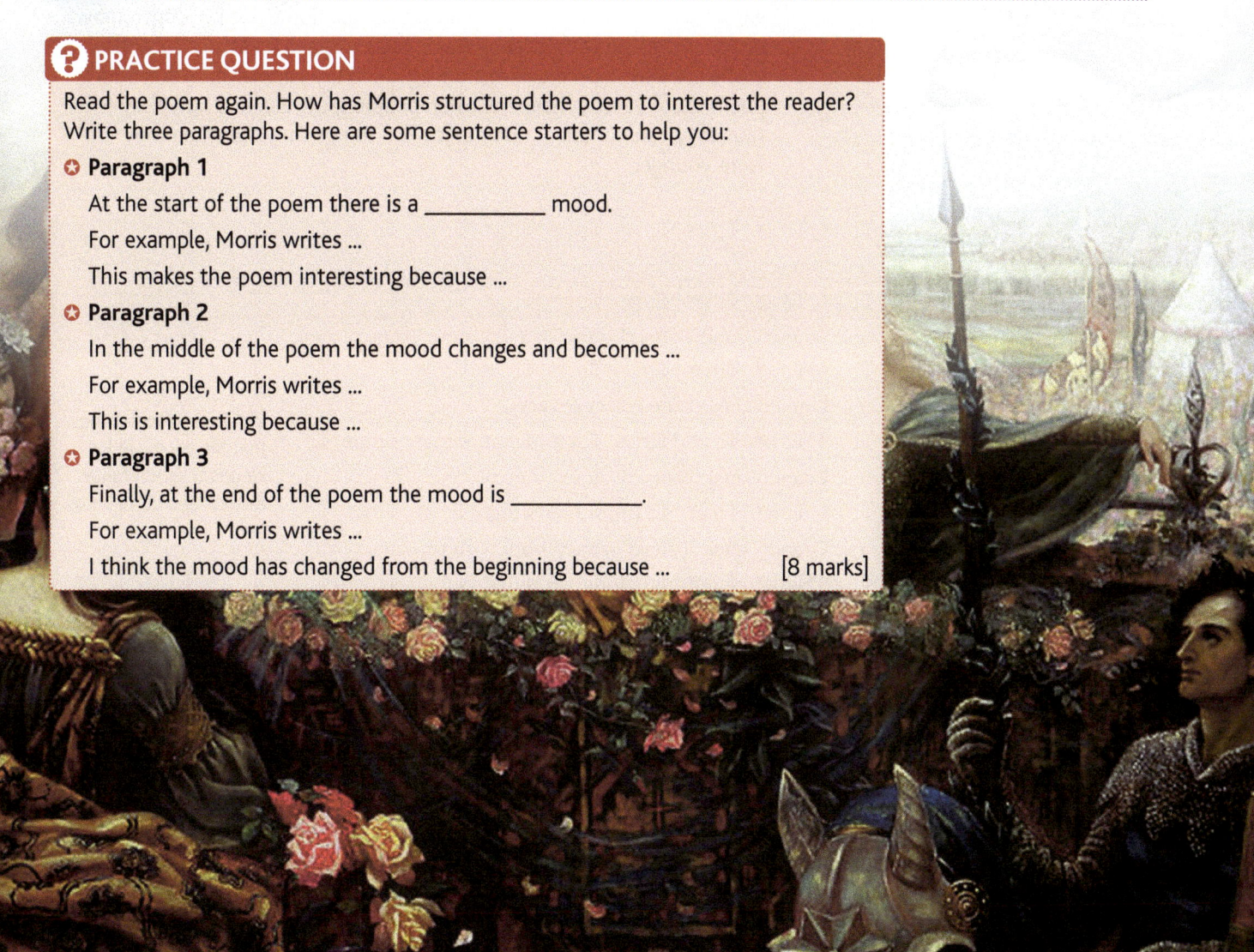

21 Ulysses

By Alfred Lord Tennyson, 1833

▲ 'Ulysses returns Chryseis to her father' by Claude Lorrain

LEARNING OBJECTIVES

- To distinguish the main ideas.
- To find and list information.
- To show awareness of how language choices affect meaning.

CONTEXT

A famous Greek myth is that of Odysseus. His Roman name was Ulysses. Odysseus was a soldier in the Trojan War who angered the god Poseidon, who was the god of the sea. As a punishment, Poseidon caused lots of storms and shipwrecks and made sure that it took Odysseus many years to get home. This poem, 'Ulysses', by Tennyson, explores our hero's emotions once he is back home. He no longer knows his family or the people he rules. He feels trapped and isolated, and wishes to leave home and explore again. Many people think that this poem is about what happens when people grow old, and how they feel that they can no longer do or enjoy the things they did when they were younger.

Tennyson uses lots of adjectives to describe how useless Ulysses feels now that he is at home and growing old.

Ulysses is drinking so much because he is sad and restless.

Tennyson uses listing to show how excited Ulysses is when he talks about his past adventures.

It little profits that an **idle king**,
By this **still hearth**, among these **barren crags**,
Match'd with an **aged wife**, I **mete** and dole
Unequal laws unto a savage race,
5   That hoard, and sleep, and feed, and know not me.
I cannot rest from travel: I will drink
Life to the **lees**: All times I have enjoy'd
Greatly, have suffer'd greatly, both with those
That loved me, and alone, on shore, and when
10 Thro' scudding drifts the rainy **Hyades**
Vext the dim sea: I am become a name;
For always roaming with a hungry heart
Much have I seen and known; cities of men
And manners, climates, councils, governments,

Ulysses is complaining that the people in his kingdom do not follow the law and don't know him.

Ulysses is always roaming as he likes adventure.

15 Myself not least, but honour'd of them all;
    And drunk delight of battle with my peers,
    Far on the ringing plains of windy Troy.
    I am a part of all that I have met;
    Yet all experience is an arch wherethro'
20 Gleams that untravell'd world whose margin fades
    For ever and forever when I move.
    How dull it is to pause, to make an end,
    To rust unburnish'd, not to shine in use!
    As tho' to breathe were life! Life piled on life
25 Were all too little, and of one to me
    Little remains: but every hour is saved
    From that eternal silence, something more,
    A bringer of new things; and vile it were
    For some three suns to store and hoard myself,
30 And this gray spirit yearning in desire
    To follow knowledge like a sinking star,
    Beyond the utmost bound of human thought.

    This is my son, mine own Telemachus,
    To whom I leave the sceptre and the isle,—
35 Well-loved of me, discerning to fulfil
    This labour, by slow prudence to make mild
    A rugged people, and thro' soft degrees
    Subdue them to the useful and the good.
    Most blameless is he, centred in the sphere
40 Of common duties, decent not to fail
    In offices of tenderness, and pay
    Meet adoration to my household gods,
    When I am gone. He works his work, I mine.

    There lies the port; the vessel puffs her sail:
45 There gloom the dark, broad seas. My mariners,
    Souls that have toil'd, and wrought, and thought with me—
    That ever with a frolic welcome took
    The thunder and the sunshine, and opposed
50 Free hearts, free foreheads —you and I are old;
    Old age hath yet his honour and his toil;
    Death closes all: but something ere the end,
    Some work of noble note, may yet be done,

Ulysses talks about how dull his life is now.

Tennyson is showing us how restless Ulysses is. He is meant to travel, not stay at home.

Ulysses is proud of his son, Telemachus.

Tennyson uses personification to show that the vessel is ready to sail.

The seas are 'dark' and 'broad' which shows that they are mysterious and dangerous.

Ulysses says his sailors are hardworking.

Ulysses starts getting hopeful. It's not too late to travel again.

Not unbecoming men that strove with Gods.
55 The lights begin to twinkle from the rocks:
The long day wanes: the slow moon climbs: the deep
Moans round with many voices. Come, my friends,
'T is not too late to seek a newer world.
60 Push off, and sitting well in order smite
The sounding furrows; for my purpose holds
To sail beyond the sunset, and the baths
Of all the western stars, until I die.
It may be that the gulfs will wash us down:
65 It may be we shall touch the Happy Isles,
And see the great Achilles, whom we knew.
Tho' much is taken, much abides; and tho'
We are not now that strength which in old days
70 Moved earth and heaven, that which we are, we are;
One equal temper of heroic hearts,
Made weak by time and fate, but strong in will
To strive, to seek, to find, and not to yield.

Ulysses wants to travel far.

Although this final journey will be difficult as Ulysses is much older, he is still excited.

GLOSSARY

Idle king: a king who has nothing to do
Still hearth: a fireplace that doesn't burn
Barren crags: cliffs and hills where nothing grows
Mete: hand out
Lees: the bottom of the barrel of wine
Hyades: nymphs who bring rain
Vext: the storms are disturbing the sea
Wherethro': through which
Unburnish'd: dull
Telemachus: Ulysses' son
Sceptre: a stick carried by rulers
Mariners: sailors
Frolic: cheerful
Achilles: a hero from the Trojan War who died in battle

SKILLS FOCUS

✔ Summarise the poem.
✔ List information from the poem.
✔ Analyse Tennyson's use of language.

LOOK CLOSER

1. Read the poem again. How do you think Ulysses is feeling? Draw a concept map outlining all of his feelings. Find a quotation for each one. For example, he complains about how his wife is now old.

2. Now write a summary of how Ulysses is feeling. Here are some sentence starters to help you:
   - At the start of the first verse, Ulysses is feeling …
   - As the verse progresses, he starts feeling …
   - In the middle of the poem, Ulysses is feeling …
   - By the end of the poem, Ulysses' mood is …

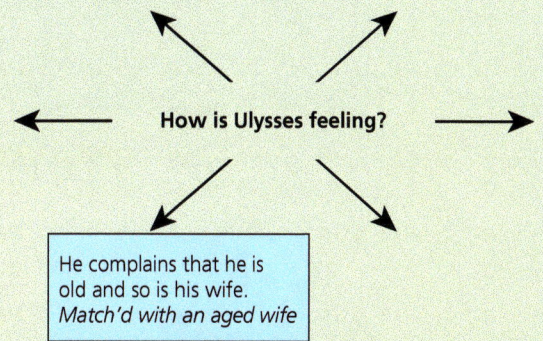

He complains that he is old and so is his wife. *Match'd with an aged wife*

FAST FINISHERS

Why do you think Ulysses is so sad? Do you think that Ulysses feels differently by the end of the poem? Give reasons for your answer.

NOW TRY THIS

1. Do some research about Ulysses (also known as Odysseus) and his home-coming, then write a diary entry from his point of view. How does he feel now that he is home? Why would he be sad? Make sure that you write in the first person. You may wish to begin your diary like this:

> Dear Diary,
> It has been years since I went on my adventures. Now I am so old and I feel so sad …

FAST FINISHERS

There is a lot of artwork based on the story of Ulysses/Odysseus. Do some research and find some information about the different artists who painted the Ulysses/Odyssey story. Write a summary of your findings.

2. In pairs, pretend one of you is an interviewer and one of you is Ulysses. Prepare a role play to present to the class. Include information about:
   - the Trojan War
   - Ulysses' journey from Troy to his home, Ithaca
   - what happened when Ulysses reached home.

PRACTICE QUESTION

Read lines 1–15 of the poem. How has Tennyson used language to show the reader how Ulysses is feeling? Consider the language features that Tennyson has used. Aim to write three paragraphs. [8 marks]

22 The Fairies
By William Allingham, 1883

▲ 'The arrival of the king and queen of fairies' by E Stuart Hardy

LEARNING OBJECTIVES
- To distinguish the main ideas and select relevant points from the texts.
- To explore mood and atmosphere.
- To show awareness of how language choices affect meaning.

CONTEXT
William Allingham was an Irish poet born in 1824. He wrote many poems and 'The Fairies' is one of his most famous. In the poem, Allingham describes a group of fairies. However, whilst many people view fairies in a positive way, this poem explores more negative and frightening aspects of fairies.

Up the airy mountain,
Down the rushy glen,
We daren't go a-hunting
For fear of little men;
Wee folk, good folk,
Trooping all together;
Green jacket, red cap,
And white owl's feather!

Down along the rocky shore
Some make their home,
They live on crispy pancakes
Of yellow tide-foam;
Some in the reeds
Of the black mountain-lake,
With frogs for their watchdogs,
All night awake.

High on the hill-top
The old King sits;

The fairies are described as 'little men'.

The men are viewed positively here.

Allingham uses adjectives to describe the fairies' home and the food they eat.

The Fairies

He is now so old and grey
He's nigh lost his wits.
With a bridge of white mist
Columbkill he crosses,
On his stately journeys
From Slieveleague to Rosses;
Or going up with the music
On cold starry nights,
To sup with the Queen
Of the gay Northern Lights.

They stole little Bridget
For seven years long;
When she came down again
Her friends were all gone.
They took her lightly back,
Between the night and morrow,
They thought that she was fast asleep,
But she was dead with sorrow.
They have kept her ever since
Deep within the lake,
On a bed of fig-leaves,
Watching till she wake.

By the craggy hillside,
Through the mosses bare,
They have planted thorn trees
For my pleasure, here and there.
Is any man so daring
As dig them up in spite,
He shall find their sharpest thorns
In his bed at night.

Up the airy mountain,
Down the rushy glen,
We daren't go a-hunting
For fear of little men;
Wee folk, good folk,
Trooping all together;
Green jacket, red cap,
And white owl's feather!

The fairy king is described as old and forgetful.

The fairy king enjoys eating with the queen.

The fairies stole little Bridget. How has the mood of the poem changed now?

The fairies do other unpleasant things, such as putting thorns in people's beds.

How do you feel about the fairies by the end of the poem?

Poetry

GLOSSARY

Airy: wide
Rushy glen: a valley covered in rushes
Yellow tide-foam: the foam from the tide of the sea
Nigh: almost
Columbkill: a place in Ireland
Slieveleague to Rosses: places in Ireland
Gay: happy

SKILLS FOCUS

✔ Understand the ideas in the poem.
✔ Analyse Allingham's use of language.
✔ Analyse the structure of the poem.

LOOK CLOSER

1 Read the poem again. Now draw a storyboard summarising what happens in the poem.

1)	2)
3)	4)

2 The poem contains some dramatic adjectives. Copy and fill in the table below analysing the effect that they have on the reader. The first row has been done for you.

Sentence	Adjectives	How does this make the reader feel?
Up the airy mountain, Down the rushy glen,	airy, rushy	Allingham is describing the vast countryside and is suggesting that the fairies are everywhere.

FAST FINISHERS

Draw up three columns headed, **Language device**, **Example** and **Effect on the reader**. Now complete this with a list of some of the other language devices used in the poem and an explanation of their effect on the reader.

The Fairies

NOW TRY THIS

1 Using the information in the poem, write your own fact file about the Old King Fairy. You could start the fact file like this:

Name of fairy	Old King Fairy	
Height		
Age		
Clothing		
Interesting features		
Special qualities		

You could finish with a drawing of the King that matches the ideas in your fact file.

FAST FINISHERS
Create your own fairy and write a fact file about it.

2 Imagine that you are walking through the Irish countryside and come face to face with some fairies.
Write the script for a chat show where a presenter interviews you about your experience. Share your interview with the rest of the class.

? PRACTICE QUESTION

Read the poem again. How has Allingham structured the poem to interest the reader? Write three paragraphs. Here are some sentence starters to help you:

- **Paragraph 1**
  At the start of the poem there is a _____ mood.
  For example, Allingham writes ...
  This makes the poem interesting because ...
- **Paragraph 2**
  In the middle of the poem the mood changes and becomes ...
  For example, Allingham writes ...
  This is interesting because ...
- **Paragraph 3**
  Finally, at the end of the poem the mood is ...
  For example, Allingham writes ...
  I think the mood has changed from the beginning because ...   [8 marks]

93

23 Beowulf
Translated by Seamus Heaney, 1999

▲ Beowulf and the dragon

LEARNING OBJECTIVES
- To distinguish the main ideas.
- To analyse the writer's use of language.
- To consider the cultural context of the poem.

CONTEXT

Beowulf is an Old English epic poem that was written between AD975 and AD1025. The entire poem is 3182 lines long. It is a very important poem as it is one of the first poems that was written in English.

The poem is about Beowulf, an Anglo-Saxon warrior, and how he helps Hrothgar, the King of the Danes, whose banqueting hall has been attacked by Grendel, a monster. Beowulf kills Grendel and Grendel's mother. After this, Beowulf goes back to Sweden and becomes King of the Geats. At the end of the poem, Beowulf defeats a dragon but dies as a result of the injuries he gets in the battle.

Nobody knows who wrote *Beowulf*. The version that we are reading has been translated by Seamus Heaney, who was a very famous Irish poet. He was born in 1939 and died in 2013. The following extract is taken from the start of *Beowulf*.

So. The **Spear-Danes** in days gone by
And the kings who ruled them had courage and greatness.
We have heard of those princes' heroic campaigns.

There was Shield Sheafson, **scourge** of many tribes,
A wrecker of **mead-benches**, **rampaging** among **foes**.
This terror of the **hall-troops** had come far.
A **foundling** to start with, he would flourish later on
As his powers waxed and his worth was proved.
In the end each clan on the outlying coasts
Beyond the **whale-road** had to yield to him
And begin to pay tribute. That was one good king.

- The ancient kings were well-respected.
- Shield Sheafson was an orphan who became a great king. Heaney uses verbs such as 'rampaging' to show how good he is in battle.
- The simple sentence here highlights what a great king he was.

Beowulf

> Afterwards a boy-child was born to Shield,
> A cub in the yard, a comfort sent
> By God to that nation. He knew what they had tholed,
> The long times and troubles they'd come through
> Without a leader; so the Lord of Life,
> The glorious Almighty, made this man renowned.
> Shield had fathered a famous son:
> Beow's name was known through the north.
> And a young prince must be prudent like that,
> Giving freely while his father lives
> So that afterwards in age when fighting starts
> Steadfast companions will stand beside him
> And hold the line. Behaviour that's admired
> Is the path to power among people everywhere.

Annotations:
- Shield's son is described as a gift from God.
- Beowulf becomes incredibly famous.
- Even when the King is on the throne, princes should be generous.
- The narrator argues that a prince must be generous and kind, then, when he becomes king, people will be loyal to him.

GLOSSARY

Spear-Danes: an ancient Danish clan
Scourge: enemy
Mead-benches: the bench at an ancient feast
Foes: enemies
Hall-troops: servants in the banqueting hall
Foundling: a baby abandoned by its parents and looked after by other people
Whale-road: the sea
Tholed: gone through
Prudent: thoughtful

SKILLS FOCUS

✔ Summarise the poem.
✔ List information from the poem.
✔ Show awareness of how context helps us understand the text.

Poetry

LOOK CLOSER

1. Read the poem again. Draw a concept map of all of the qualities that make a good king. Find a quotation for each one. For example, they have to be brave.

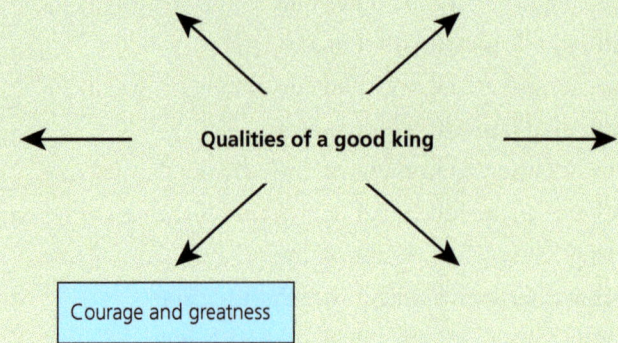

2. What differences are there between being a ruler during Beowulf's time and being a ruler now? Copy and fill in the table below outlining the differences.

A ruler then	A ruler now
A ruler had to have courage in battle.	Rulers no longer fight in battles.
The ruler set an example for his people to follow.	

3. Another character in *Beowulf* is Grendel, a monster. Do some research on Grendel and then fill in the table below:

Appearance	
Personality	
Qualities	
Behaviour	

FAST FINISHERS

Do some research on *Beowulf*. What happens in the rest of the poem? What was life like at the time the poem was first written? Why do you think that it was written? Write three paragraphs summarising your research.

Beowulf

NOW TRY THIS

1. Who is your favourite leader? Is it someone you know, possibly from your school, or is it someone from history? Write three paragraphs describing them and outlining why you think that they are a brilliant leader.

   FAST FINISHERS
   Draw an advert for the film version of *Beowulf*. Make sure that you include the following in your poster:
   - persuasive language encouraging people to watch the film
   - some information about the plot
   - information about the actor playing Beowulf
   - a dramatic picture.

2. Pretend you are Beowulf. Write a speech praising your father. Make sure that you include the following in your speech:
   - an engaging opening
   - the qualities that make a good ruler
   - a memorable ending.

   Once you have written and rehearsed your speech, share it with the rest of the class.

3. There are many different versions of *Beowulf*, including artwork, comics and films. Research some different versions of *Beowulf* and share your findings with the rest of the class.

? PRACTICE QUESTION

Read the extract of the poem again. List four things we learn about Beowulf. [4 marks]

24 Mrs Midas

By Carol Ann Duffy, 1999

LEARNING OBJECTIVES

- To make inferences about characters.
- To comment on writers' presentation of characters, using evidence from the text.
- To explore writers' techniques.

CONTEXT

In Greek mythology, King Midas was a man who was granted a wish: everything he touched turned to gold (see Extract 7). This extract is from a poem written by Carol Ann Duffy, which explores the story of Midas from the point of view of his wife. Mrs Midas is sad as her husband can no longer do basic things such as eat or drink. He also can't touch his wife as, if does so, she will turn to gold. The poem is set in modern times rather than long ago, which makes it comical. Carol Ann Duffy is a very famous British poet who was born in 1955. 'Mrs Midas' is from an anthology called *The World's Wife*, where Duffy retells traditional myths from the point of view of the men's forgotten wives.

▲ 'King Midas with his daughter' by Walter Crane

> Mrs Midas is cooking. Duffy has used personification to describe the steam going on the windows.

> Duffy describes the first time Mrs Midas sees her husband touch something which turns to gold.

It was late September. I'd just poured a glass of wine, begun to unwind, while the vegetables cooked. The kitchen filled with the smell of itself, relaxed, its steamy breath gently blanching the windows. So I opened one, then with my fingers wiped the other's glass like a brow. He was standing under the pear tree snapping a twig.

Now the garden was long and the visibility poor, the way the dark of the ground seems to drink the light of the sky, but that twig in his hand was gold. And then he plucked a pear from a branch. – we grew Fondante d'Automne – and it sat in his palm, like a lightbulb. On. I thought to myself, Is he putting fairy lights in the tree?

> Duffy uses a rhetorical question to describe the confusion Mrs Midas is feeling at present.

Mrs Midas

> Mrs Midas is thinking about a history lesson she had at school about kings who exchanged cloths of gold

> She is starting to panic because everything is turning into gold. Her husband just laughs.

> Midas cannot eat as his food is turning to gold.

> Duffy uses humour here. Mrs Midas doesn't mind having a gold toilet.

> Midas has to give up smoking as his cigarettes turn to gold too.

He came into the house. The doorknobs gleamed.
He drew the blinds. You know the mind; I thought of
the Field of the Cloth of Gold and of Miss Macready.
He sat in that chair like a king on a burnished throne.
The look on his face was strange, wild, vain. I said,
What in the name of God is going on? He started to laugh.

I served up the meal. For starters, corn on the cob.
Within seconds he was spitting out the teeth of the rich.
He toyed with his spoon, then mine, then with the knives, the forks.
He asked where was the wine. I poured with a shaking hand
a fragrant, bone-dry white from Italy, then watched
as he picked up the glass, goblet, golden chalice, drank.

It was then that I started to scream. He sank to his knees.
After we'd both calmed down, I finished the wine
on my own, hearing him out. I made him sit
on the other side of the room and keep his hands to himself.
I locked the cat in the cellar. I moved the phone.
The toilet I didn't mind. I couldn't believe my ears:

how he'd had a wish. Look, we all have wishes; granted.
But who has wishes granted? Him. Do you know about gold?
It feeds no one; aurum, soft, untarnishable; slakes
no thirst. He tried to light a cigarette; I gazed, entranced,
as the blue flame played on its luteous stem. At least,
I said, you'll be able to give up smoking for good.

> The doorknobs are gleaming because they have turned into gold.

> Mrs Midas' hand is starting to shake because she is afraid of her husband.

> The glass Midas is drinking from and its contents turn to gold, which means he cannot drink.

> Mrs Midas doesn't let her husband touch anything as she doesn't want anything else to turn into gold.

> She discusses the disadvantages of having gold: it doesn't feed anyone or provide drink.

GLOSSARY

Fondante d'Automne: a type of pear
Aurum: the Latin word for gold
Slakes: satisfies
Luteous: the colour of the flame

SKILLS FOCUS

✔ Understand and summarise events in the poem.
✔ Analyse Duffy's use of language.
✔ Explore the character of Mrs Midas.

Poetry

LOOK CLOSER

1 Read the poem again. Now copy and fill in the table below summarising what happens in each stanza. The first stanza has been done for you.

Stanza	Summary
1	It is late September. Mrs Midas is cooking and watching her husband who is in the garden.
2	
3	
4	
5	
6	

2 Now use your table to draw a storyboard of the poem. You will need to have six boxes on your storyboard, one for each of the events you just identified.

3 Copy and complete the table below analysing some of the language features that Duffy uses in the first part of the poem and how this makes the reader feel.

Vocabulary	Language feature	How does this make the reader feel?
The kitchen filled with the smell of itself, relaxed, its steamy breath gently blanching the windows	Personification	
He sat in that chair like a king on a burnished throne.	Simile	
then watched as he picked up the glass, goblet, golden chalice, drank.	Three-part list	
I locked the cat in the cellar. I moved the phone. The toilet I didn't mind.	Humour	

Mrs Midas

Vocabulary	Language feature	How does this make the reader feel?
Look we all have wishes; granted. But who has wishes granted? Him. Do you know about gold?	Rhetorical questions	

FAST FINISHERS
Analyse the language features that Duffy uses later on in the poem.

NOW TRY THIS

1 Using the information in this part of the poem, write a diary entry for Mrs Midas. How does she feel about her husband? You may start your diary like this:

> Dear Diary,
>
> My husband is such a greedy fool! You won't believe what he has just done …

Make sure that you write using first person narrative and that you use paragraphs when writing your diary.

FAST FINISHERS
Duffy has set this poem in the modern day, using a conversational, chatty style. This makes it funnier and also makes us feel empathy towards Mrs Midas.

Choose another poem that you have studied in this anthology. Retell it from a modern perspective. Before you write your new poem, think about:
- the point of view that you are going to use
- the language devices you will include
- the structure of your poem.

2 Do you think that Mrs Midas is right to be angry with her husband? As a class, prepare a debate about this. Half of the class agree that Mrs Midas should be angry. The other half of the class disagree. Your teacher will decide who has won the debate.

PRACTICE QUESTION

Read the poem again. How has Duffy used language to explore the character of Mrs Midas? Write at least three paragraphs in response. Here are some sentence starters to help you with your first paragraph:
- Firstly, Duffy uses …
- For example, she writes …
- This makes the poem interesting because …

[8 marks]

Key terms

Active verb	When the person or thing does something, rather than has an action done to them.
Adjective	A word that describes a noun, e.g. the reckless man.
Adverb	A word that describes a verb, e.g. he ran hastily.
Alliteration	When two or more words begin with the same letter or sound, e.g. 'Jolly giant giraffes jest joyfully in June'.
Anecdote	A story from the writer's own personal experience.
Bildungsroman	A story told from a young character's point of view which charts their development as they change and grow.
Compare	To find similar qualities between ideas.
Context	Background information about the writer or the time the text is set.
Contrast	To have very different qualities to something else.
Dialogue	A conversation between two or more people.
Dramatic irony	When the significance of the character's words or actions is clear to the audience but unknown to the character.
Ellipsis	A set of dots that usually indicates a pause or that words have been intentionally missed out. (Note: the plural is ellipses.)
Emotive language	Language that appeals to a reader's emotions.
End rhyme	Rhyme between a poem's line endings.
Explicit information	Information that is stated clearly.
Figurative language	Language such as similes, metaphors or personification.
Foreshadowing	When later events in a story are hinted at before they happen.
Imagery	The use of language to create word pictures by comparing one thing with another; see also metaphor, personification, simile
Imperative	A command or request.
Implicit information	Information that is implied, rather than stated clearly.
Internal rhyme	Rhyme that occurs within a single line of a poem.
Juxtaposition	Putting two contrasting ideas next to each other.
Metaphor	When a word or phrase is used to describe something else, e.g. 'She was on fire', to suggest that she is very good at what she is doing.
Mood	The atmosphere of a piece of writing, e.g. scary, peaceful, exciting, dull, sad.
Narrative approach	First person (I walked), second person (You walked) or third person (He/She/They walked).
Noun	An object, e.g. chair; name, e.g. Sarah; or emotion, e.g. love.
Onomatopoeia	When a word sounds like the sound it describes, e.g. Bang!
Paraphrase	Expressing the meaning of something by using different words.
Pathetic fallacy	Where the weather (or other inanimate object) reflects what is happening in a story.
Personification	Describing something that isn't human by using human qualities, e.g. 'The tree danced in the wind'.
Pronoun	A word used in place of a noun or someone's name, e.g. I, you, she, they, my, our, themselves.
Protagonist	One of the major characters in a story.
Quotation	Taking a group of words from a text or speech.
Repetition	Repeating a word or phrase to make it memorable.
Rhetorical question	A question in writing or speech that is used to involve the reader but does not require an answer.
Sibilance	The repetition of 's' sounds for effect, e.g. 'The sly and sinister snake'.
Simile	When something is compared to something else using the words 'like' or 'as', e.g. 'As snug as a bug', 'Cold like ice'.
Tone	The attitude of a writer towards the subject or his audience, e.g. funny, sad, formal, informal, sarcastic.
Verb	An action word, e.g. running, walked, dances.